The Sacred Foodways of Film

The Sacred Foodways of Film

Theological Servings in 11 Food Films

Michael, 'kain na!'
TON S.

Antonio D. Sison

PICKWICK *Publications* · Eugene, Oregon

THE SACRED FOODWAYS OF FILM
Theological Servings in 11 Food Films

Pickwick Publications
An Imprint of Wipf and Stock Publishers
199 W. 8th Ave., Suite 3
Eugene, OR 97401

www.wipfandstock.com

PAPERBACK ISBN 13: 978-1-4982-3046-9
HARDCOVER ISBN 13: 978-1-4982-3048-3

Cataloguing-in-Publication Data

Sison, Antonio D.

The sacred foodways of film : theological servings in 11 food films / Antonio D. Sison.

x + 118 p. ; 23 cm. Includes bibliographical references.

ISBN: 978-1-4982-3046-9 (paperback) | ISBN: 978-1-4982-3048-3 (hardback)

1. Motion pictures—Food. 2. Food—Religious aspects. 3. Motion pictures—Religious aspects. I. Title.

PN1995.5 S33 2016

Manufactured in the U.S.A.   02/17/2016

To my mother Josephine David Sison,
and my late grandmother Germana Cunanan David,
women of faith and fortitude
who nourished their families
with inspired meals
cooked from the heart.

Contents

Acknowledgments

Heartfelt thanks to all who contributed ingredients that made their way into the cooking process of *The Sacred Foodways of Film*:

My Catholic Theological Union colleagues Dianne Bergant, Steve Bevans, Laurie Brink, Gil Ostdiek, and Don Senior for generously sharing reference materials, and for the helpful suggestions; and Melody Layton-McMahon and Richard Mauney for the copy-editing and technical help.

Supportive friend Corey Knapke for screening food films with me, CPPS housemate Loi Nguyen for the thoughtful gestures and the flavorful Vietnamese dishes, and CPPS co-pilgrim Joe Grilliot for the continuing table fellowship.

My sister Patty Sison-Arroyo and my brother-in-law Laurence Arroyo, who have, in my seasonal visits to the other shore, earnestly shared my passion for scholarship over scrumptious meals of *sisig*.

And special thanks to Pickwick Publications of Wipf and Stock Publishers for the trust and support.

Introduction

SINIGANG (SEE-NEE-GAHNG) IS A symphonic combo of tomatoes, water spinach, string beans, taro, and a protein of pork belly pieces or fish and shrimp, afloat in a tamarind sour soup, and usually complemented with the subtle, aromatic notes of guava. It is best served piping hot, lightly drizzled with fermented fish sauce or dark soy sauce, and eaten with fragrant *milagrosa* or jasmine rice. Filipino chefs and food experts have identified the flavors and cooking technique of *sinigang* to be precolonial, the dish that comes closest to representing indigenous Philippine culinary culture. The use of a sour-fruit soup base, for one, not only offered the flavorful acidity to counterbalance the tropical climate, it was also a way of preserving food in humid conditions. It is not in the least surprising that *sinigang* is one of the few dishes that are considered customary fare in households across the archipelago. To be sure, Filipinos are not the only fans of the dish. "Stunningly clean, elegant, and fresh tasting," is the verdict of *Esquire* UK food writer Tom Parker-Bowles while sampling a bowl of *sinigang* prepared by a noted Filipino chef. "And the sourness is just right," he adds. "Simple yet glorious."[1]

As a US immigrant from the Philippines, *sinigang* for me is "simple yet glorious" in a sense that goes beyond taste. It is an

1. Tom Parker-Bowles, "Anyone for Filipino?," 87.

1

edible time-travelling portal of sorts, one that leads me back to memories of a specific personal experience when, as a college student in Manila, I tasted transcendent goodness in a serving of *sinigang*.[2] It was the monsoon season, heavy downpours had flooded the city's arteries. I was stranded for two hours, waiting for a ride home after my evening classes. When I was finally able to wrestle my way into a packed jeepney,[3] the best it could do was literally inch its way through the horrendous traffic jams. Another two hours had passed and we still had some two miles to go before my bus stop. Frustrated, I decided to negotiate the remaining stretch on foot. Motored by necessity and a prayer, I braved the relentless monsoon rains and walked the dark flooded streets until I finally landed at the entrance of our house at 11:00 PM. I was drenched to the bone and dead tired. And I was hungry. Very hungry. After a shower and a change of clothes, I sat at the dining table and there was the comforting sight of my mother, ladling the pork *sinigang* she had cooked into a serving bowl. Gifted with intuition and creativity, my mother cooks from heirloom recipes she inherited from her own mother. Not one of them written on paper, she learned these recipes by observation and participation; they are inscribed in the cookbook of her memory.

2. While watching an episode of the TV cooking competition *Top Chef*, I had a strong emotional response when Sheldon Simeon, a Hawaii-based chef of Filipino ancestry, won the "restaurant wars" challenge with a fine dining version of *sinigang*. Sheldon holds vivid memories of his grandfather Urbano's *sinigang*, something that he truly relished as a young boy growing up in the Philippines. Naming his restaurant concept "Urbano," he honored his grandfather's memory in the dish that he cooked. One of the judges, a noted restaurateur, recognized the soul in Sheldon's *sinigang*: "This flavor kinda makes you sit up straight. . . in a good way. It's very, very clear that Sheldon is cooking from his heart."

3. The jeepney is the ubiquitous public transport vehicle that plies the streets of Metropolitan Manila and most cities in the Philippines. The first jeepneys were US military jeeps that had been re-purposed in the aftermath of World War II.

© 2015 Pia Sison

It does not take much to imagine how my mother's delicious *sinigang*, served on a particularly wearisome night, would be for me a taste of divine goodness. "Bless us, O Lord, and these, thy gifts, which we are about to receive from thy bounty, through Christ our Lord. . ." I prayed, and unlike the rote manner by which I had been saying grace since childhood, I prayed from the heart that night and meant the "Amen." Bar none, I still consider it as the best meal I've ever had. Not just because it was prepared by a gifted cook, but more so because it was the culinary expression of the nourishing love and care that could've only come from my own mother. And this could not have been appreciated more than on that dark and stormy night when my singular wish was simply to get home.

Born and raised in a country where cooking and feasting are wedded with ancient communitarian values such as *pagmamagandang loob* (heartfelt hospitality) and *pakikisama* (heartfelt solidarity), part of my identity draws from the food memories cooked in the pot of the culture that first formed me. While not always apparent, these have been my bread-crumb trails to the foodways that enriched my understanding of the nourishing presence of the sacred.

THEOLOGICAL SERVINGS IN FOOD FILMS

Food and eating have a well-established place in Scripture, both in the material/physiological sense as nourishment for the body, and in the metaphorical sense as the idiom for spiritual sustenance. To be sure, the Bible blurs the distinction between these two senses. The Psalmist likens putting one's faith in God to savoring food. God's goodness is so real that it is akin to one of the most essential of human sensory experiences. "O taste and see that the Lord is good; happy are those who take refuge in him." (Psalm 34:8) The gospels, of course, are replete with food metaphors. Besides hosting what could arguably be the greatest banquet in human history when he multiplies five loaves and two fish to feed thousands (Matthew 14:13–21; Mark 6:31–44; Luke 9: 10–17; John 6:5–15), Jesus identifies himself as the "bread of life" (John 6:35), and in his final Passover meal, shares bread and wine—"for my flesh is true food and my blood is true drink" (John 6:53–55)—with his disciples. Like heirloom recipes handed down from one generation to the next, the food metaphors from Scripture have given nourishment and life to Christian theology and spirituality, and there is not a dearth of written sources on the subject.

Film, particularly, the genre of "food film," has been helpful in offering creative spaces for deeper insight on food and eating. Judging from the list of iconic titles that are considered to be part of a "canon" of food films—notably *Tampopo* (Juzo Itami, Japan, 1985), *Babette's Feast* (Gabriel Axel, Denmark, 1986), *Like Water for Chocolate* (Alfonso Arau, Mexico, 1992), *The Scent of Green Papaya* (Tran Anh Hung, France/Vietnam, 1993), *Eat Drink Man Woman* (Ang Lee, Taiwan, 1994), and *Big Night* (Campbell Scott, Stanley Tucci, USA, 1996)—the link between food and the depth dimension of the human journey have found ample cinematic representation. To begin with, film as an art form lends itself quite well to the representation of food in that its audiovisual language and grammar bridge our consciousness with our senses. The combination of stylistic options—cinematography, editing, mise-en-scène (props, sets, settings, lighting, acting), music, and dialogue—conspire to create evocative scenes of undeniable visceral power, allowing us to sit as omnipresent partakers of meals served at various dinner tables; this often whets our appetite for actual food, a real feeling of hunger. In film and mind studies, this cinematic phenomenon has been identified as a "sensory/affective fusion."[4] Said differently, it is the film wielding its magic, making us almost smell and savor the food images we see onscreen so that by the time the culinary genius Babette Hersant, protagonist of *Babette's Feast*, serves rum-infused yeast cake with dried figs, the luscious dessert of her multi-course gourmet French dinner, we are ready to head to our favorite restaurant and obey our hunger! Indeed, the visual is the visceral. Correspondingly, film, in its capacity to represent human stories of which food figures decisively, invites a conversation about the delicate turns where food and faith dovetail. In my previous work, I commented on how a film like *Babette's Feast* draws us to recognize "theological conversation points" arising from our encounter with the cinematic portrayal of vivid humanity, "like a quest for eternal treasure in jars of clay."[5] I add that these interpretive impulses seethe and bubble in the very food images depicted onscreen. The cinematic representation of food becomes *locus theologicus*, a site for theological discovery and insight. In essence, this represents a "pro-active acknowledgement of the sacramental power of film as art."[6]

The Sacred Foodways of Film is my open-minded theological engagement with such films. The interpretive journey consists of three key considerations. First, I abstain from using the uncritical "add theology and mix" approach and allow film, in its autonomy as an art form, to invite me to discover theological currents through

---

4. In its original application, the term sensory/affective fusion was used by Colin McGinn to refer to the power of cinematic dream imagery to elicit powerful affect. *The Power of Movies*, 103–6.

5. Sison, *World Cinema, Theology, and the Human*, 5–6.

6. Ibid., 5–6.

an inductive process. This means that preconceived theological frameworks are initially bracketed so that film is allowed to speak on its own terms. The nodal points (to borrow a term from photography), those junctures where film and theology line-up and resonate with each other, are identified in the process of navigating through the film's artful layers. The fuller theological integration is reserved until after I have completed the cinematic homework. This leads to the second consideration. Careful attention is given to the stylistic, audiovisual dimension of cinematic storytelling and not simply to the literary elements such as theme, plot, and dialogue. As I noted earlier, the visceral power of food imagery works particularly well in an audiovisual idiom so that ignoring this cinematic aspect would be an ironic oversight indeed.[7] Lastly, the notion of "foodways" serves as a critical lens through which the representation of food in film is seen and explored. First registering on the academic radar in 1970s and developing in the areas of cultural anthropology and folkloric studies,[8] the term "foodways" refers to the multiple channels by which food and food-related activities mirror and shape sociopolitical, cultural, and religious identity and relations. It is complex in its range, covering "the beliefs and behaviors surrounding the production, distribution, and consumption of food."[9] The foodways approach is of great value in examining food in its multiform dimensions, whether material, cultural, or aesthetic, precisely because we do not simply source, cook, and eat food. We source, cook, and eat food "as"... as members of a family and a community of support and accountability, as native informants thoroughly formed by our cultural histories, as sexual beings defined by gender roles, as representatives of social and professional circles, and as this book emphasizes, as people of faith who understand food not simply as bodily nourishment but as sacramental disclosures of a reality larger than ourselves. The

7. Scholars in the field of Religion and Film have long advocated for the examination of film *qua* film, not as a mere adjunct to literature. Sison, *World Cinema, Theology, and the Human*, 5–6.

8. Baron, et al., *Appetites and Anxieties*, 17.

9. Counihan, *Anthropology of Food and the Body*, 2.

critical lens of foodways provides a wider and deeper aperture in the analysis of the contextual meaning of food in film, and in the drill down, allows for a reasoned and creative gleaning of theological insight.

The first chapter "Are you Hungry?" considers three popular film titles and enters into a discussion of food by way of negation, that is, through the shortage or absence of food. Here, the meaningful web of human relationships offers clarifying touchstones to a deeper understanding of the phenomenon of hunger. If eating is meant to be a communal act, then hunger can be indexical of human isolation. The first two titles invite a discussion of hunger in its interpersonal dimension. *Into the Wild* (Sean Penn, USA, 2007) is a cinematic re-telling of the true story of Christopher Mc-Candless, a free-spirited young man who turns his back on the trappings of "the world" and the false securities it offers, and sets out on a road trip to bare subsistence living. Hiking and hitchhiking from one town to the next until he ends up in the untamed wilderness of Alaska, McCandless realizes that in his self-imposed exile, he had starved himself of food and of vital human relationships. *127 Hours* (Danny Boyle, USA/UK, 2010), could well be the flipside of *Into the Wild* in that it is also based on true events in the life of another adventurous lone ranger, Aron Ralston, who, on a solo adventure trek in Utah's Blue John Canyon, accidentally gets trapped in a rocky crevice. Dangerously deprived of food and water, he realizes on hindsight that staying connected with family and friends would've given him the lifeline that he needed. Unlike McCandless, Ralston is blessed with a redemptive moment and lives to tell the tale. The third title *Angela's Ashes* (Alan Parker, USA, Ireland, 1999), another film based on an autobiographical narrative, kindles a discussion on the social-religious dimension of hunger. Set in the impoverished town of Limerick in Midwest Ireland during the 1930s, the young boy Frank McCourt is in a bleak social milieu characterized by joblessness, tuberculosis, and hunger. Adding insult to injury, the local Catholic pastors fail to provide McCourt and his family with adequate nourishment, whether of the bodily or spiritual sort. The issue of hunger raises important questions on the dangerous memory of the historical Jesus, the eschatological prophet who feeds the hungry; and the ethical imperative of the Reign of God.

A natural segue from the theme of hunger is the ongoing human quest for daily bread, a term that is iconic of any other type of staple food that a given community consumes for subsistence. Entitled "Fishing, Gleaning, and 'Eatripping,'" chapter two examines three documentaries and reflects on how the Lord's prayer— "Give us this day our daily bread" (Luke 11:3)—is both grace and responsibility. In *ICHTHUS* (Ton Sison, Philippines, 2006), a short theological art film I lensed on a shoestring, the gospel account of the multiplication of the loaves and fish is inculturated in the folk Catholic storytelling culture of a poor fishing village in Lingayen, a town northwest of the Philippine capital of Manila. In the face of a meager catch that needs to be distributed to a number of fisher folk and their families, I ask the question "How can such a great love give so little?" *The Gleaners and I* (Agnès Varda, France, 2000) echoes a similar question but from the perspective of an "internal third world" in France where people at the margins glean from the spillage of commercial over-production. Here, theology offers a critique of the surplus mentality of capitalism that, at base, evinces a lack of faith in God's providence. The Japanese documentary *Eatrip* (Yuri Nomura, Japan, 2009), a reflective look at how a diverse group of people is re-discovering the spirit of food in its essential, organic forms, serves as a closing doxological piece to the chapter.

The significance of culinary culture—in this case, the ancient cuisine of India—as custodian of authentic identity, is the thematic interest of the third chapter "Identity Simmers in the Cooking Pot." The Indian film *The Lunchbox* (Ritesh Batra, India, 2013), recipient of critical acclaim and standing ovations in the international film festival circuit, centers on a young housewife in a loveless marriage that relegates her to a servile status. Preparing packed lunches for her unappreciative husband each day, she begins to dream of an alternative life-giving reality for herself when Mumbai's lunchbox delivery system, which is noted for its sterling service record, delivers her lunch to the wrong office address and serendipitously connects her to a semi-retired widower. Symbolically expressed in culinary scenes, the rediscovery of self-worth and mutuality in her life dovetails with the quest for women's full humanity, a critical principle in feminist theology. While authentic gender identity is of special interest in *The Lunchbox*, authentic cultural identity is the thematic focus of *The Hundred-Foot Journey* (Lasse Hallström, USA, 2014), a crowd-pleaser produced by Steven Spielberg and Oprah Winfrey. A migrant family from Mumbai settles in a small French town and puts up an Indian restaurant just a hundred feet across from a Michelin-starred French restaurant. As an inevitable clash of cultures breaks out, a gifted young chef finds renewed inspiration in the food memories associated with his late mother who taught him the foodways of Indian culture. Quasi-religious undertones, specifically in the meaningful connection between food and memory, share subtle resonances with the Christian Eucharistic meal.

The fourth chapter "Eating at the Table of Finitude" is a reflection of the role of foodways as human life approaches its end. The first of two titles in this chapter is *A Simple Life* (Anne Hui, Hong Kong, 2011), an affecting contemplation on the relationship between a bachelor and an elderly housekeeper who has been serving his family for the better part of sixty years. Practically raising him from infancy, the housekeeper continues to care for her now middle-aged master, meticulously preparing special dishes for him each day. When she suffers a stroke and has to move to a home for senior living, a reversal of roles ensues; he gets the chance to expresses his gratitude and care for her by paying regular visits and taking her out to restaurant meals. The second film is *Departures* (Takita Yôjirô, Japan, 2008), winner of the 81st Oscar Award for Best Foreign Language film. A cellist is forced to accept a job as a *nōkanfu*, a traditional Japanese ritual encoffiner or mortician, when the orchestra he is playing for declares bankruptcy. Food and meals play a significant role in affirming life as the encoffiner and his colleagues encounter the somber reality of death on a regular basis. Theological reflection centers on the link between our need to eat and our creaturely mortality, how we, as members of the human community, all have a place at the table of human finitude, and how there is great dignity in the passage from life to death and to renewed life in the hereafter.

Finally, I devote the last chapter to a single film, *Beasts of the Southern Wild* (Benh Zeitlin, USA, 2012). A mytho-poetic tale told from the perspective of an inspirited six-year-old girl, *Beasts of the Southern Wild* is set in a fictional island on the Louisiana bayou that is reeling in the aftermath of a Katrina-force perfect storm. The deceptively small film has a cosmic scale that eludes a singular, conclusive interpretation, but there is no denying that food and feasting figure prominently in the protagonist's vital relationships—with ultimate reality, with nature, with her community, with her estranged mother, with her dying father, and with herself. Entitled "The Buffet of the Universe," the chapter is an engagement with these conversational threads in the light of a Christian eschatological perspective, within which reconciliation, cinematically expressed in the grace inherent in food and feasting, serves as a unifying theme.

While this book owes much to the previously mentioned canon of food films and the abundance of accompanying scholarly work about them, the filmography here consists of more recent, critically recognized titles of global cinema that offer fresh insight to the discussion table. It is worth mentioning that the films spotlighted in each of the chapters are commercially available on either DVD or Blu-Ray, or on popular online streaming sources such as Amazon and Netflix (my own short film *ICHTHUS* is uploaded on Vimeo). Readers have the option to view the films at their convenience and come to a more meaningful engagement with the intertextual character of this book. This is especially helpful when a film with a rich symbolic matrix such as *Beasts of the Southern Wild* is brought into the spotlight and analyzed.

Smithsonian magazine describes the last two decades as "The Era of Crazed Oral Gratification."[10] The explosion of interest in food culture, or what is touted as the "foodie revolution,"

10. Rosenbaum, "Anthony Bourdain's Theory on the Foodie Revolution," para. 1.

is evident across media platforms in the United States as well as in other parts of the world. From blockbuster movies such as *Julie and Julia* (Nora Ephron, 2009), *Eat Pray Love* (Ryan Murphy, 2010), and *Chef* (John Favreau, 2014); documentaries such as *Jiro Dreams of Sushi* (David Gelb, 2011), *Spinning Plates* (Joseph Levy, 2012), and *Step Up to the Plate* (Paul Lacoste, 2012); television reality shows such as *Top Chef, The Chew, Hell's Kitchen, Iron Chef,* and Anthony Bourdain's *No Reservation* and *Parts Unknown;* to popular books that are too numerous to mention, the "foodie revolution" has reached fever pitch. The scholarly interdiscipline of food and film has kept up with the pace of the food phenomenon. Now on its second edition, Steve Zimmerman's *Food in the Movies* (2010) catalogs, in a patient accumulation of detail, memorable food scenes from the silent era to the present. Looking at the food film from the optic of genre studies, James R. Keller's *Food, Film and Culture: A Genre Study* (2006) examines culinary imagery and its relationship with cultural constructs such as politics, ethnicity, and gender. Cynthia Baron, Diane Carson, and Mark Bernard's co-authored *Appetites and Anxieties: Food, Film, and the Politics of Representation* (2013) is an ideological analysis of the representation of foodways in both fiction and documentary films.

Curiously, there has not been a book specifically dedicated to the confluence of theology/religion and food films. *The Sacred Foodways of Film* is a timely contribution to this fascinating area of interest that has long been simmering on the stovetop of scholarship. Over and above proposing reasoned entry points to a deeper, more reflected understanding of food films, my hope is that in the open-minded engagement with the creative contours of film, readers would taste and see the goodness of the Sacred.

1

Are You Hungry?

Into the Wild
127 Hours
Angela's Ashes

AS SNEAKY AS A church mouse, the orphan boy darts into the dining room, snatches slices of bread and a glass of wine, and scurries furtively up the stairs to the attic. Neither does he eat of the bread nor drink of the wine, the meal is for Jesus Christ himself miraculously made flesh from a life-size wooden crucifix. What motivates the boy is simple. Jesus had responded affirmatively to a straightforward question he asked earlier: *Tienes hambre?* ("Are you hungry?").

The scene is from *Marcelino Pan y Vino* (literally "Marcelino Bread and Wine," Ladislao Vajda, Spain/Italy, 1955), a film whose bare-faced folk piety, realistically speaking, limits its appeal to Sunday School and traditional Catholic circles. Be that as it may, it is interesting that Marcelino asks Jesus—here, presumably and necessarily "true man"—a key anthropological question. Whether an expression of care routinely asked by a mother to her children, or one that is posed by a social worker to a homeless person, "Are you hungry?" taps into one of the most primal and universal of human experiences, one that demands, for obvious reasons, an immediate response. The representation of hunger is the unambiguous interest of this chapter, fully aware that our approach to food and film here is by negation, that is, by way of a close examination of films that portray the failure to satisfy this most basic of human needs. But as members of the human family interconnected in a matrix of relationships, it is necessary for us to pay close attention to hunger as a more complex phenomenon, that is, as an experience that could be brought about by a breakdown of our significant relational synapses, both on a personal level and on a larger social context, rather than a mere shortage or absence of food. First, we bring to sharper focus the experience of hunger as a result of a failure of interpersonal relationships. In the spotlight is the critically acclaimed popular film *Into the Wild* (Sean Penn, USA, 2007), and, as an integrative coda, the equally noted British independent film *127 Hours* (Danny Boyle, UK, 2010). Both titles were shortlisted by the American Film Institute (AFI) as one of the best ten films of their respective years of release. We then look into hunger within the frame of a socio-religious context as we examine the film *Angela's Ashes* (Alan Parker, UK/Ireland, 1999), winner of the Irish Film and Television Awards Best Picture Award for the year 2000.

I AM HUNGRY

Into the Wild tells the story of Christopher McCandless, an idealistic 20-year-old Emory University graduate who literally abandons everything he has—family, money, law school prospects, middle-class comforts—on course to a noble, albeit misguided, pilgrimage toward a purer life of utter simplicity. *127 Hours* details the heroic fight for survival of Aron Ralston, a 27-year old hiker who is trapped between boulders in a deserted canyon. As they share compelling resonances, there is good reason to bring these two films together. *Into the Wild* and *127 Hours* are film versions of published, true-to-life biographies. The protagonists in the two films have very similar character profiles, both McCandless and Ralston are young outdoorsmen with a dauntless can-do idealism. And of specific interest to our project is the representation of hunger in these films, both of which drawing the link between the protagonists' experience of starvation and the cracks in their relationships with members of their own family. However, the two characters' respective responses to their circumstantial backgrounds fork to different outcomes, but to say anything further at this point would be putting the carriage before the horse. That said, let's take a closer look at the hungry protagonist in *Into the Wild* and from there, segue to *127 Hours*.

Into the Wild easily grafts onto the "road movie" genre. We follow Christopher McCandless—self-reinvented as a sojourner named "Alexander Supertramp"—as he hikes and hitchhikes from one loosely determined stop to the next. Although his ultimate goal is to reach the Alaskan wilderness, it is not so much a destination-driven journey for Supertramp as it is a protracted walkout from the career rat race, crass consumerism, empty politics, and superficial social expectations that, for him, characterize American society in general. It is also his clear break from his dysfunctional parents who are in a turbulent marriage. The young sojourner meets various folks along the way who develop a sincere fondness for him. Supertramp is at once naïve and wise, impulsive and grounded, free-spirited and dogmatic, contradictions that make him naturally interesting and attractive. On one hand, he is the reckless daredevil, defying the law to paddle across the perilous rapids of an angry river; on the other hand, he is the strict moralist who refuses the "come hither" advances of a sixteen-year-old Lolita.

As can be expected from an extended journey with scant provisions, food figures constantly in the film's storyline. This is dramatized in an early scene where Supertramp is shown enjoying an apple while sitting in solitude on a bridge during a rest stop.

From Into the Wild © 2008 Paramount Home Entertainment

Framed in a medium shot, he is good-naturedly reciting an ode to the fast disappearing fruit in-between covetous bites:

> SUPERTRAMP: You're really good. You're like a hundred thousand times better than any apple I've ever had. I'm not Superman, I'm Supertramp. . . you're Super Apple. You're so tasty, you're so. . . organic, you're so natural. You're the apple of my eye!

It really is a very simple scene yet it stands out as one of the most joyful, exuberant images in *Into the Wild*. The backdrop, a beautiful cascading waterfall internally framed by the concrete balusters of the bridge, works collaboratively to convey a sense of celebration, while the accompanying music, Eddie Vedder's uplifting song "Rise," provides the aural validation. It is reasonable to propose that there is a quasi-religious sensibility in this meaning-laden representation of the simple joy of eating an apple, an indirect appeal to a divinely created world in the extolling of an often overlooked, perfectly natural food. In *Food and Faith: A Theology of Eating*, Norman Wirzba speaks of eating as an affirmation of the blessedness of creation:

> Eating reminds us that we participate in a grace-saturated world, a blessed creation worthy of attention, care, and celebration. . . Real food, the food that is the source of creaturely health and delight, is precious because it is a fundamental means through which God's nurture and love for the whole of creation are expressed.[1]

1. Wirzba, *Food & Faith*, 2.

Supertramp's paean to a natural world that offers the gift of food may be seen as an audiovisual doxology, a form of affirmation for a created world that is sacramental. Sublimated in the praises for creation is a loving Creator who is infinitely gracious. "It is divine love made food, made life for man (human beings)."[2]

That the center of attention in the scene is an apple confirms the significant import of food, and, conversely, the absence thereof, as a central motif in the film. Scene after scene, we see Supertramp passing through the agrarian landscape of wheat fields, combine harvesters, and grain bins; he is surrounded by food being grown and produced. At one point, he even ends up, ironically, flipping burgers at Burger King. As he enters wild territory, Supertramp begins to depend on gathering and hunting for his daily sustenance.

From Into the Wild © 2008 Paramount Home Entertainment

On a split screen, a stylistic strategy where two simultaneous scenes unfold on a single screen space, we see him foraging for wild berries on one screen, and tightening his belt on the other. The belt-tightening is a continuing motif in the film, evidently indicating that Supertramp is progressively losing body mass. We also see split screen images of him shooting some small mammal and roasting it, dressing a bird, and catching a fish. He is now in survival mode. In one poignant scene, Supertramp shoots a large moose and begins field dressing the downed animal, a task that turns out to be way more challenging than the instructions he scribbled previously on his notebook. As he dresses the ponderous

2. Schmemman, *For the Life of the World*, 14.

carcass, Supertramp is assaulted by the carnage of raw flesh, viscera, fur, and blood. And when he finally has the pieces of meat ready, he fails to keep the swarms of flies away despite his desperate efforts; we see close-ups of crawling maggots now eating away on the raw meat. The scene serves as a foreboding of how the daily search for food in the unforgiving wilderness will prove to be a losing battle for Supertramp.

At a later turn, the hard reality that food has become scarce overtakes Supertramp and sends him to the brink of madness; he is starving and food is nowhere in sight. In a wide-angle shot, we see him standing by the river on a small island of gravel, shooting randomly up in the air with his rifle in a fit of desperation:

> SUPERTRAMP: Where are the f_cking animals now!?
> I'm hungry! I'm f_cking hungry! I'm f_cking hungry!

The scene is the key to a deeper understanding of Supertramp's experience. It serves as an iconic representation of the ultimate reason for his starvation that ultimately lies in his self-imposed exile from vital human relationships. Supertramp had marooned himself in a deserted island, beyond the reach of his family and friends who have, in one form or another, offered him lifelines. In not just one occasion, he received standing invitations to stay connected, including a proposal for adoption from the elderly Ronald Franz who was very fond of him. Incontestably, the core of Supertramp's alienation is his separation from his own family, who all this time, had been left in the dark about his whereabouts. We see vignettes of his parents, perceptibly remorseful, as they bear the open wound left by their son's absence. In a melancholic interlude, his mother sets the dinner table and then pauses halfway, reminded that her son would not be there to share the meal with them. "Are you hungry?" could well be her unspoken wondering about her missing son, an agonizing primal concern for any mother.

Towards the latter part of the film, we see Supertramp practically reduced to skin and bones. Acutely starved, he consults his catalogue of wild plants and forages for a wild potato root, which, in the end, turns out to be poisonous. When he consults his catalogue of wild plants, his tragic fate is revealed in the close-up shots of the text that reads, "digestive system. . . starvation. . . death." In the throngs of death, images of himself reconciling with his parents flash before him. He then scribbles something on a blank space of a book page and the cryptic message reads: "Happiness real when shared." There have been conflicting reports about the actual cause of his death but perhaps it is reasonable to say that he–Christopher McCandless–died of hunger. For food. For human relationship. Theologically, Wirzba describes the folly of "eating in exile" in terms that so chillingly resonates with the experience of McCandless in the film that it could well serve as a sort of epitaph of the tragedy of his experience:

> The truth, of course, is that none of us can stand alone. To try is invariably to flail about and fall. It is also to die by starvation. Each of us is held in "creatureliness" through the multiple food webs that constitute and circulate through every living organism. Eating is the daily confirmation that we need others and are vulnerable to them. . . But when we eat in exile we eat alone and with considerable violence, without deep connection or affection, experiencing food and each other as mere objects and threats or as the means to our power, control, and convenience.[3]

As an integrative companion piece to *Into the Wild*, I draw attention to *127 Hours*, another cinematic dramatization of a true-to-life story. Unlike the former, Danny Boyle's film is upbeat from the outset; it opens with a frenetic triple screen featuring various images of crowds of people engaged in a variety of shared activities—audience clapping, sports fans cheering, swimmers in a race, etc.—before one of the screens show the contrastingly solitary images of protagonist Aron Ralston (James Franco) getting his gears and supplies ready. Ralston is setting out on a journey that is markedly different from McCandless's existential, often brooding, pilgrimage; he is going up to Utah's Blue John Canyon on an adventure trek. He is so pumped up for the trek that he ignores

3. Wirzba, *Food & Faith*, 77.

phone messages left in his answering machine. A drive and a bike ride after, Ralston is scaling the heights of the arid canyon and enjoying his solitude amid the breathtaking natural landscape. He meets a couple of women hikers on the way and he leads them to a fun plunge between a rock crevice, into a clear natural spring. All the exuberant energy would come to an abrupt halt when Ralston finds himself lodged in a crevice not unlike the one he just had fun sliding through; a boulder had pinned his arm following an accidental slip and he is trapped in a deserted spot of the canyon. Water and food run out soon enough and he reaches a point where he eats his own contact lenses and drinks his own urine.

Uncertain about his prospects for survival, Ralston is compelled to do some soul-searching. Using his video camera as a visual journal, he records his thoughts as they come. He expresses regret for his selfishness, wishing he had informed family and friends of his plans beforehand. Twice, he apologizes to his mother for not answering her phone calls. We also see the images of family and friends that flash intermittently in his mind. It is chilling that as a consequence of Ralston's disconnect with the people who matter to him, he ends up talking to his own image on the LCD screen of his camcorder. Interestingly, he pushes away the screen at some point because it freaks him out to see himself. And in one particular scene, Ralston's recordings appear as Q&A vignettes from a mock one-man comedy talk show, identifying himself as Aron from "Loser Canyon, Utah." As he parodies the folly of his own egocentricism—"I'm a big f_cking hard hero, I can do everything on my own"—we hear the ironic sound of canned laughter. Ralston comes to realize that had he been more relational in his outlook, he would have informed somebody about his trek, help would have come, and he would have been saved from thirst and starvation, indeed, from impending death. Clearly, we can appreciate the affinity between *127 Hours* and *Into the Wild*. Both Ralston and McCandless learn from the school of hunger that we are beings-in-relation. That we are not alone. That we are saved in and by community. That "happiness is real when shared."

In an act of unbelievable courage and determination, Ralston agonizingly slices off his own arm inch-by-inch. When he finally severs the arm, he wraps the open wound with some clothing, staggers to liberate himself, and, walks some distance before bumping into hikers who quickly offer him water to drink and summon for help. He had survived the ordeal. In the film's ending, we see underwater shots of Ralston swimming in a pool, a portion of his right arm now visibly missing. As he emerges from the water, a moving sight greets him—gathered before him on a couch by the poolside are his family and close friends, gazing at him lovingly.

An allusion to the film's ending had already been presented at an earlier turn when, as in *Into the Wild*, *127 Hours* employs the stylistic option of a split screen.

From Into the Wild © 2011 Fox Searchlight

On one screen, Ralston is shown peering through a crevice on the rock; on the other screen is his family and friends seated on a couch and gazing at him.

In *127 Hours*, Ralston does not die of starvation. He pays the price of his own arm and gets another chance to bond more meaningfully with his loved ones. In *Into the Wild*, McCandless, in a manner of speaking, also finds some kind of reconciliation with his loved ones. But nature and time caught up with him and he had to pay the price of his own life. He had simply starved for too long.

WE ARE HUNGRY

Angela's Ashes, the cinematic re-telling of the bestselling autobiography by Frank McCourt, relates the story of McCourt's childhood, which was characterized by dire poverty. The film opens in Depression era Brooklyn where the McCourt couple, Malachy Sr. and Angela, struggle to support their brood of four children. When their fifth and newly born daughter dies, Angela falls into a state of depression and Malachy, an alcoholic, simply fails to be the stronger half. In desperation, the couple decides to return to Angela's hometown of Limerick in Midwest Ireland, a move that only compounds their impoverished existence. It's the 1930s and Ireland, Limerick most especially, is in pretty bad shape economically. Diseases such as the "galloping consumption" (tuberculosis) and typhoid have not been controlled, and the squalid living conditions and constantly damp weather do not help. Food is scarce and the children are plagued by hunger. In other words, Limerick is a cul-de-sac.

As in the book, the film tells the story from the perspective of Frank McCourt's adolescent self who peppers the otherwise bleak atmosphere with wit and dark humor. This does not, however, dilute the tragedy of gnawing hunger that Frank and his family experience. There simply isn't enough to eat, both in terms of quantity and quality. Scene after scene, we see them living a hand-to-mouth existence, scrounging around for food wherever they can. In one scene, while searching for his drunken father in a bar, Frank steals leftover bread from a passed out customer and wolfs it down. In another scene, he greedily licks his uncle's leftover chips stuck on a newspaper wrap. In characteristic dark humor, Frank narrates, "I was so hungry. I sat there and licked the front pages and all the headlines." Still in another scene, we are assaulted by a close-up of a grotesque sheep's head floating in a pot of gruel, the family's

Christmas dinner. Malachy scoops out the eye and, much to the horror of the children, gobbles it up it with mock gusto.

From Angela's Ashes © 2000 Paramount Home Entertainment

In *Angela's Ashes*, the situation of hunger is equated with both personal and social dimensions. Undoubtedly, there is an immediate link between the hunger of the McCourt family and the alcoholism of Malachy; he is simply an immature, irresponsible father. Given that Malachy is largely at fault, it is, however, not just about him. Widening the aperture, Ireland was saddled with grave unemployment; there was a scarcity of jobs for men and no real jobs for women except housework, and based on the film's depiction, Limerick was particularly "god-forsaken." In fact, "god-forsaken" is an apt description considering that the institutional Catholic church at the time acted more as a stumbling block rather than a rock for the faithful. In it's insensitivity for the plight of the poor who fill their pews and listen to guilt-driven sermons, the local church of Limerick "took Jesus away" so that Frank did not know where to find him. The contrast between the poverty and disease of the slums and well-provided, secure life within the walls of the church is dramatized in a couple of scenes. At one turn, the young Frank sees his mother pushing her way to receive scraps from the priests. He laments:

> FRANK: Begging for leftovers is worse than the dole, worse than the St. Vincent De Paul Charity. This is my own mother begging. This is the worst kind of shame, begging for the leftovers from the priests' dinner.

The disconnect between the message of the church and the constant hunger Frank and his family experience finds eloquent expression and indictment when the young boy writes about it for a school composition, the assigned theme being "what's it going to be like if our Lord had grown up in Limerick, the holiest city in Ireland." Giving it the title "Jesus and the Weather," Frank is ordered to read his essay as traditional printed images of scenes from Jesus' life, presumably from picture Bibles or prayer books, appear as flash cuts:

> FRANK: I don't think that Jesus, who is our Lord, would have liked the weather in Limerick because it's always raining and the Shannon keeps the whole city damp. My father says that the Shannon is a killer river because it killed my two brothers. When you look at pictures of Jesus, he's always wondering around ancient Israel in a sheet. It never rains there, and you never hear of anyone coughing, or getting the consumption, or anything like that. And no one has a job there, all they do is stand around, eat manna, shake their fists, and go to crucifixions. Any time Jesus got hungry, all he had to do was to walk up the road to a fig tree or an orange tree and have his fill. Or if he wanted a pint, all he had to do was to wave his hand over the glass and there was the pint. Or he could visit Mary Magdalene or his sister Martha and they'd give him dinner, no questions asked. So it's a good thing that Jesus decided to be born Jewish in that nice, warm place because if he were born in Limerick, he'd catch the consumption, and be dead in a month, and there wouldn't be any Catholic church, and we wouldn't have to write compositions about him.

Inadvertently, Frank's essay critiques the church's failure to bridge the gospel message with the harsh, concrete realities of poverty and hunger that most members of its flock live in.

In a more direct manner, the religious of Limerick are shown to be accomplices in the perpetuation of social discrimination. Upon the prodding of his teacher, Frank and his mother knock on the door of the "Christian Brothers" to explore the possibility of advancing his education with their help but with one look at their low-class appearance, the Brother-director simply slams the door on them without a thought. Curiously, even the lay Catholics have mercilessly contributed to the hunger of the McCourt family; steeped in a historically rooted anti-Protestant sentiment, employers refuse to hire Malachy for the reason that his accent reveals his northern Protestant origins.

There did not seem to be hope in sight for the McCourt family, especially when World War II breaks out and Malachy gets enlisted in England never to return. Only when the nineteen-year-old Frank sets out for the United States, using money he appropriates from a creditor whom he finds dead one day, is there any promise of an end to his long-drawn experience of hunger. In *Angela's Ashes*, hunger is a result of a grace-killing "conspiracy" that is at once personal, social, and religious. For the young Frank who has been hungry all his life, there is no other viable option but to seek greener pastures elsewhere and, for the meantime, eat the food of hope.

A MIRACLE OF MULTIPLICATION

Through our encounter with films that depict hunger as a central problematic; first, on an interpersonal level as represented in *Into the Wild* and *127 Hours*, and second, on a social-religious level as dramatized in *Angela's Ashes,* we are able to connect with the phenomenon in some visceral way and come to a meaningful theological reflection. I draw attention to the "Miracle of Five Loaves and Two Fish" (Feeding of the Five Thousand), the only miracle story apart from Jesus' resurrection that is present in all four gospels. According to the Johannine account, a crowd had gathered to see Jesus after he had withdrawn to the mountain for some solitude. Concerned that the people were hungry, Jesus asks his disciples where they could buy provisions to feed them and the puzzled Philip exclaims that "two hundred day's wages" won't be enough to for a crowd numbering five thousand. When Andrew mentions that one boy brought five loaves and two fish, Jesus takes them, gives thanks, and then distributes the food so that everyone has more than enough. No one is left hungry. At the end of the meal, there are twelve baskets full of fragments.

Taking into account the words and deeds of the Jesus of the Gospels, scholars have been able to propose an understanding of a central theological symbol that is never exactly defined by Jesus yet is mentioned by him ninety times at different junctures of the gospels.[4] *Basilea tou theou,* the Kingdom or Reign of God, which is described by Jesus paradoxically as "close at hand" but "not yet," refers to the holistic vision of a created world that is reconciled and made whole. It is a future eschatological reality that lies ultimately in God's hands, but already experienced here and now, albeit in fragments, whenever human flourishing is affirmed. It is clear in the gospels that Jesus is consummately identified with the Reign of God precisely because he is the Reign in person or the *autobasileia,*[5] as the Church Father Origen beautifully describes him. When Jesus desires to alleviate the hunger of the crowd of people who had gathered around him and performs the miracle of multiplication, it is a sign that the Reign of God has been brought near to humanity through the person of Jesus. He is being *autobasileia.* He is being himself.

It is worth noting that the first-century Eastern Mediterranean world of Jesus differs greatly from the contemporary milieux of the films we had just discussed; society then was community-oriented and folks were "wired" to be in relation with one another. Such a psychological orientation is known as "dyadism" (from the Greek "dyad," meaning "pair"); the typical person in Jesus' time had a dyadic personality, he or she always identified with the

---

4. Ratzinger, *Jesus of Nazareth,* 97.

5. Origen, *Commentary on Matthew* (books 12:34f. and 14:7) as cited in O'Collins, *Jesus,* 23. See also Ratzinger, *Jesus of Nazareth,* 49; and Boff, *Jesus Christ Liberator,* 133.

collective.[6] On the other hand, our film protagonists McCandless and Ralston, coming from a strongly individualistic American society, have to be intentional about staying in relation and it takes an extreme experience of hunger to call their attention to it. Surely, they have much to learn from first-century Mediterranean society.

In addition, it is quite apparent that the miracle of multiplication touches not only on the personal dimension but even more so, the social dimension. At the very core of Jesus saving action in this story is a miracle of sharing among people who live in a situation of scarcity. Studies derived from social anthropology reveal that society in Jesus' Palestine was characterized by the notion of "limited good," that is, a situation where all goods—food most especially—are in limited supply and already distributed. The pie, so to speak, does not grow larger, so that if an individual bites off a slice that is disproportionately larger than the rest, it would mean that everybody else eats a smaller portion. From this lens, we can see the profound sharing that undergirds the feeding of the multitude in John's gospel. It is a sign that in the fulfillment of the Reign of God, no one will go hungry, everyone will have more than enough. This holds special resonance for the situation of hunger portrayed in *Angela's Ashes* because in the film, the church seems to have preached a Jesus detached from the plight of the poor who do not have enough to eat, a Jesus so different from the one who, upon seeing the hunger of the multitude, gave them food to eat through a profound miracle of sharing. Jesus, the *autobasileia*, could not stand to see people not having enough to eat.

Surely, our cinematic and theological exploration of hunger raises some very important ethical challenges for us as individuals and for the community of faith. In his book *Hunger: An Unnatural History,* Sharman Apt Russell writes about Irish President Mary Robinson's firsthand encounter with starving people in Somalia and the ethical questions that shook her:

> In 1992, the President of Ireland, Mary Robinson, visited
> Baidoa, Somalia. She sat beside a woman too weak to lift
> the small bundle of her child, a sick baby with sores and

6. Malina, *The New Testament World,* 67.

flies crawling over his mouth and eyes. At a press confer-
ence, Robinson spoke emotionally, "I have an inner sense
of justice. It has been deeply offended. . . I felt shamed by
what I saw, shamed, shamed. . . What are we doing that
we have not got a greater conscience?"[7]

There are people who live in impoverished regions of the world, a
collective Economics professor Paul Collier refers to as "the bottom billion,"[8] where hunger continues to be a day-to-day reality. A
billion people suffer from malnutrition. Small children subsist on
one meager meal a day, perhaps two if they're lucky.

When the Reign of God comes to fulfillment at the oppor-
tune moment, "there will be no more thirst or hunger" (Rev. 7:16
NRSV). It will be a mode of existence that is truly and definitively
grace-saturated. In the reality of the meantime, as we allow ourselves to be nourished by the hope-inspiring vision of the Reign
and commit to a praxis of sharing, we continue to ask ourselves
and each other what the boy in *Marcelino Pan y Vino* asked Jesus:
"Are you hungry?"

7. Russell, *Hunger*, 228

8. Collier, *The Bottom Billion*, 3–14.

2

Fishing, Gleaning, and "Eatripping"

ICHTHUS
The Gleaners and I
Eatrip

THE QUESTION OF HUNGER, so mundane yet so vital, marked the previous chapter with an open-endedness that rightfully implores some form of response. That said, we pick up from where we left to explore how cinema, in its own unique language and grammar, has journeyed toward an answer as it images the universal, never-ending human quest for daily bread. . . or daily rice, maize, potatoes, beans, yams, or any other type of food that a given community consumes for subsistence. Further, we set out to explore how that quest, from the perspective of theology, is both grace and responsibility; a combo of ingredients that comes from both the gratuitous abundance of God's hand, and the diligent work of human hands. This is the one instance when the case studies that figure into the discussion are not categorized under feature-length, narrative fiction; two of the films are documentaries, the other, a short film. The reason for this is straightforward: the selected titles spotlight "daily bread" in a thematic and stylistic way that invites a compelling interface with relevant theological insights. The first title is *ICHTHUS*,[1] a 2006 short digital art film I wrote, shot, directed, and produced on a shoestring. Blurring documentary and fiction boundaries in what I would describe as a quasi-documentary, *ICHTHUS* is a mytho-poetic re-telling of the gospel accounts of the multiplication of five loaves and two fish re-situated in a poor fishing village in the Philippines, my country of birth. The film asks a hard theological question—"How can such great love give so little?"—that reverberates through regions of the globe where eating three square meals a day remains a hard fought battle for survival. The second title is the 2000 film *The Gleaners and I*, a good-natured documentary lensed by Agnès Varda, the only woman filmmaker associated with the French *nouvelle vague* film movement of the 50s and 60s. Armed with a handheld videocam, Varda travels to the margins of French society in search of people who gather discarded surplus and scraps from potato fields, vineyards, orchards, and markets, and in the process, gleans some thoughtful reflections on thrift and wastefulness in a milieu of plenty. Finally we look into the 2009 Japanese film *Eatrip*, a cinematic meditation on the profound connection between food, nature, and people, all gathered together at the table in the daily ritual of eating.

THE PARABLE OF THE HALF-EATEN FISH

For the people of the coastal town of Lingayen in the northwestern Philippines, the real name of the peculiar fish known in English as tongue sole is *kera-kera'y diyos*, which literally translates as "God's leftovers." As a child, I had first encountered the fish on the beach when I accidentally discovered a juvenile specimen in the shallows, camouflaged in a small mound on the wet grey sand.

---

1. *ICHTHUS* is available for online viewing: https://vimeo.com/139267591.

Looking at the fish's unusual body—flat and tongue-like with both eyes set on one side, and a nondescript flipside—the name made sense. The fisherfolk figured that God ate half of the fish, the other half he left for humans to eat, thus the fish's odd "half-eaten" appearance. Further sleuthing, however, made me realize that there is another version to the *kera-kera'y diyos* story, a deeper, more parabolic story. Somewhere between the fish's unusual morphology and the resonance of the Gospels stories in the predominantly Catholic islands, a profound parable explaining the divine origins of this fish had arisen in the local culture as oral tradition. It became apparent to me that "God's leftovers" does not quite capture the true force of meaning behind *kera-kera'y diyos*; the more meaningful dynamic equivalent would be "God-given portion."

From ICHTHUS © 2006 Antonio Sison

"*Kera-kera'y diyos* does not merely represent the discarded scraps from Jesus' table, rather, it is an inspired gift which has its origins in the very heart of the God of the edge who is ever mindful of the poor and downtrodden. Here is my imaginative re-creation of the story:

> Jesus sees that the people who had gathered around him to listen to his teachings were tired and hungry. He knew that most of them were poor and had barely enough to make ends meet yet they had come because

they hungered for God's word. Moved by compassion, Jesus asks if anyone had food to share. His apostles were perplexed about the question, wondering how anyone could have enough food to feed such a big crowd. But a small boy steps forward and gives Jesus what he had: a small fish. Taking the boy's fish, Jesus looks up to heaven and says a prayer of thanksgiving. He then divides the fish into two equal parts. The first half, he multiplies and distributes to the crowd so that everyone could eat to their heart's content. The other half, he revivifies with his breath of life, and releases back into the sea. Time and tide bring the fish to multiply and all of its offspring take the form of a half-fish, a sign celebrating the memory of a small boy and his profound act of sharing. Through this miracle of multiplication, Jesus makes certain that the poor of generations to come would have enough to eat. It is their God-given portion.

Inadvertently, the townsfolk had appropriated the miracle story of the multiplication of the fish and loaves found in all four canonical gospels—Matthew 14:13–21; 15:32–29; Mark 6:31–44, 8:1–9; Luke 9:10–17; and John 6:5–15—and inculturated it to apply meaningfully to their context. But that is not all. The story and the fish also symbolize a faith that continues to believe in the super-abundance of God's grace amid poverty and hardship. My encounter with *kera-kera'y diyos* as a child was the germ of an idea for a future theological art film, a short mockumentary that came to be titled *ICHTHUS,* the Greek word for "fish," whose five letters *Iota, Chi, Theta, Upsilon, Sigma* stand for the words *Iesous Christos, Theou Uios, Soter,* or "Jesus Christ, Son of God, Savior." I was not so much interested in recording events as they unfolded, I wanted to take a deeper, more reflective focus on reality and share through the eyes of my camera what I had seen. As a native informant, that is, someone born and raised in the Philippines, I had questions. Hard questions.

The film opens with an angelophany, the main character Jonas sees an angel in a dream. This is rendered impressionistically in the film; a luminous, half-exposed face of the heavenly being is intercut with close-ups of the sleeping Jonas. The angel brings a message: "The sea will birth a miracle. . . a multiplication of fish here and now. Look for the fish called ICHTHUS." Immediately, a montage of fish swim into the frame of Jonas' dream, the anticipation of a miraculous catch. But this is rudely interrupted when menacing sharks make an appearance leaving Jonas, now awakened from sleep, pondering what all these might mean. On a breadcrumb trail to the miracle, Jonas travels back to his hometown in search of clues to the mysterious ICHTHUS. His mother, a wise woman with an uncanny sense of intuition, accompanies him to the fish market and points to strange-looking flatfish called *kera-kera'y diyos*. Jonas loses no time in tracking back where the fish had come from and finds himself in Lingayen Gulf, the very beach where he spent happy weekends as a child. Just shortly after the break of dawn, the beach is already abuzz with activity. Adult men are pushing their *bancas* or wooden outrigger boats out to the open sea in preparation for *kalukur*, a local fishing method involving the hauling-in of fishing nets that have been cast into the deep. Women await the catch of fish, which they will sort and then sell at the market. Older children look after their younger siblings while their parents immerse themselves in the day's work. In this scene, wide-angle shots capture the movement and energy of the communitarian dance; the quest for the day's food has begun.

The hauling-in of the net from the shore is a slow, labored process, and when the load of fish is finally brought in, it is not a big catch by any stretch of the imagination.

From ICHTHUS © 2006 Antonio Sison

As we see the women sorting the fish for the market, the camera reveals that the last batch of fish consists of *kera-kera'y diyos*. Jonas is disheartened about the catch, it falls short of the fishing miracle revealed to him by the angel in his dream. On an even deeper level, he is disappointed with God.

> JONAS: Your leftover fish? Is this the ICHTHUS miracle? How can such great love give so little? Your children remain poor. There is no ICHTHUS.

As Jonas laments, we see a montage of ocean debris that had been washed ashore, metaphorically dramatizing that if anything, what Jesus had given the fisherfolk were scraps from his table, not a miraculous catch of fish.

I intentionally created the character Jonas to serve as my cinematic alter ego. He is my eyes, ears, and heart. Jonas's lamentation, in fact, is my own. As a Filipino who had grown up in a milieu where a multitude live in reduced circumstances, it is but natural for me to lament the fact that there are regions in my country where the manna for the day does not fall from heaven but has to be struggled for and earned "fish per fish" through a never-ending

33

cycle of backbreaking work. In shooting this film, I followed the trail to the market where I found out for myself that the fish sold for a pittance; for my shooting purposes, I had purchased a dozen fish for the equivalent of US$1.50. Compounding the situation is the very unpredictability of the sea that guarantees neither a bountiful catch, nor safety for the fisherman. In his poem "Ode to the Sea," Pablo Neruda, the Chilean Nobel Prize laureate for literature, captures the precarious day-to-day life of poor fishermen who have to navigate through the untamed currents of the sea that is both their friend and foe. In spite of this, they still find fortitude and hope, believing that at the heart of their struggles is "our daily bread, our fish, and our miracle."[2] The fishermen's prayer—that the sea would bless them with their "daily fish"—is the very prayer of the fishing community of Lingayen who, notwithstanding hardships, believes that "the sea is life" (in the vernacular: *say dayat bilay*), the watchword emblazoned on one of the fishing boats. The resonance with Neruda's prayer-poetry takes on a particular poignancy when we consider the harsh conditions within which the Lingayen fisherfolk have to live. A typical home for them is a cramped bamboo-and-straw hut with neither electricity nor running water, and with the very beach sand for flooring. Bar none, all of us need to find ways of obtaining the daily bread we need in order to live, "Anyone who has never toiled in order to eat has missed a basic human experience."[3] But the plain-spoken fact is that not everyone lives in a land of milk and honey. Not a few members of the human family still have to make great sacrifices just to be able to feed themselves and their families. And for people who depend directly on nature for sustenance, theological questions are especially inevitable. How can a God of super-abundance square with the reality of human toil and hardship where entire communities have barely enough to eat? How can God not cross the boundary on behalf of this poor fishing village? They are not asking for fancy gourmet dinners and fine wines. They are not asking for amply stocked pantries filled not just with the basics but with cookies and

2. Neruda, *Love*, 41.

3. Barbotin, *The Humanity of Man*, 322.

sweets and ice cream and chips of every flavor. All they ask for is a good catch so that their families will be filled for the day. How can a prayer so reasonable be denied? "How can such a great love give so little?" These questions do not arise from a lack of faith; on the contrary, they arise from the heartcry of a struggling people who have nothing but faith.

The tide of the following day brings some clarity to Jonas when Bunjo, a mysterious fisherman he had met in his childhood, makes an unexpected appearance. The enigmatic Bunjo offers a pithy reminder:

> BUNJO: ICHTHUS is half a miracle. We are the other
> half. And a little child shall lead us.

In the film, the clue to what promises to be the answer had been symbolized in the very parable of *kera-kera'y diyos*. The ICHTHUS miracle is one of partnership and collaboration; a marriage of divine and human agency. The fisherfolk who hold the other half of the fish are themselves the miracles they have been waiting for. For sure, the answer is not spelled out categorically but allusively. The sincere, luminous smiles on the faces of the children, captured in close-up, are thresholds of an inner and an outer; an innate dignity emanates from the deep end of the human heart. There is promise and possibility that has yet to be fished. But a more universal "we," all of us in the human family, also hold the other half of the fish. Drawing wisdom from the parable of the multiplication of the loaves and fish, the miracle of multiplication is very much a miracle of sharing. What then does the ICHTHUS miracle mean for those of us who live in societies where food is multiplied to a surfeit of choices while others in many parts of the world consider themselves blessed to be able to eat one full meal a day. . . two if they are extremely lucky? Surely, the answer is in our hands.

THE HEART OF GLEANING

From a poor fishing community in what is designated as the global south, we move to the affluent north where, ironically, some people continue to live in an "internal third world" where they are left with little choice but to forage for a bite to eat each day through the overspill of production and consumerism. *The Gleaners and I* begins at the Orsay Museum in Paris with a close-up of *The Gleaners*, an 1857 painting by French painter Jean-François Millet. A trickle of museum visitors takes turns gazing at the painting; by extension, we the audience see what they see. The painting features three women peasants in a field, backs bent over to glean from the remnants of a grain harvest. In the distant background are farm workers amid stacks of hay, telling us that indeed, the scene captured on canvass occurs at post-harvest. Millet's painting becomes the starting point of filmmaker's Agnès Varda's sojourn to the fringes of French society in search of people who subsists on the age-old activity of gleaning.

The scene that follows serves as a prologue for the film, a montage that features gleaners foraging for their daily bread in both rural and urban environs. Rap music with pointed lyrics plays through the montage:

> Yeah, food grub
> It's bad, sad, man
> To bend down is not to beg
> But when I see them sway
> My heart hurts!
> Eating that scrap-crap
> They've got to live on sh_t bits
> They've got to frisk for tidbits
> Left on the street, leftovers
> Rough stuff with no owners
> Picking up trash like the streetsweeper
> Zero for us, for them much better
> They've got to roam around
> To kill the hunger
> It's always been the same pain
> Will always be the same game

Like watching a "road movie," we follow Varda travelling from one locale to another to interact and converse with people who glean for their daily bread. The first stop is a potato field that had just been harvested. Tons of potatoes are being sorted and graded in a processing facility while trucks take the rejects—tubers that had grown bigger than the marketable size range of 2–4 inches or had been damaged—to a specified area in the field where they dump them. Farm managers explain that they harvest 4,500 tons of potatoes every season, 25 tons of which are rejected. Wide-angle shots reveal the obscenely vast amounts of dumped potatoes left out in the open to rot. Disproportionately, only a bare handful of gleaners make an appearance at the site. A couple of young boys, accompanied by their mother with a baby in her arms, happily fill plastic bags with potatoes as they sing:

> Monday, potatoes
> Tuesday, potatoes
> Wednesday, potatoes again
> Thursday, potatoes
> Friday, potatoes
> Saturday, potatoes again
> Sunday, potatoes *au gratin*

Through its playful melody and lyrics, the ditty has a sad and ironic undercurrent–what is being dumped by commercial over-production is the daily bread this family and countless other people need to live. The scene takes on added poignancy because the unwitting commentary comes from innocent and vulnerable children who deserve an additional claim to food and sustenance. Another gleaner, a middle-aged man, loads sacks of about 200–300 pounds of large potatoes into the trunk of his station wagon. As he fills a sack, he mentions that some of them are misshapen, some, strangely heart-shaped.

From The Gleaners and I © 2002 Zeitgeist Video

The heart-shaped potatoes trigger excitement in Varda who quick-ly films them with her hand-held videocam, and then films them again after she brings them home with her.

Her close-up shots spark a noble idea—to get the Good Heart Charity Meals to glean on the day the potatoes are dumped. We then see a couple of volunteer members–a single mother and a man in between jobs—who themselves are beneficiaries of the Charity, filling bags with potatoes. In the time they spend gleaning, their haul amounts to 700 pounds. Soon after, a trailer-dwelling gypsy makes an appearance and estimates that there are nearly a ton of potatoes in the several mounds that are in the fields, and he is tak-ing home a mere 70 pounds. "Disgraceful" is how he describes the wastefulness. Varda's camera further dramatizes the man's lament, framing him in such a way that countless potatoes form the back-drop as he speaks.

Varda's itinerary includes stops at a wine vineyard, a fig or-chard, and a vegetable plantation that all prohibit gleaning in the name of business interests. At this juncture, a middle-aged man dressed in the robes of a barrister stands in a patch of abandoned cabbages and gives a short lecture on the rights of the poor to glean in fields. To substantiate this position, he refers to his "Bible," the penal code, which indicates two conditions for gleaning: 1) that it is legal from sunrise to sundown; 2) that it should be done only after harvest. He further refers to an edict dating back to November 2, 1554 stipulating the right of the poor, wretched, and deprived, to glean. I submit that there is an even more ancient legal and moral basis for gleaning that can be found in the very pages of the Hebrew Bible:

> When you reap the harvest of your land, you shall not reap to the very edges of your field, or gather the gleanings of your harvest. You shall not strip your vineyard bare, or gather the fallen grapes of your vineyard; you shall leave them for the poor and for the alien: I am the Lord your God.
>
> Leviticus 19:9–10 NRSV

An abridged version of the same law is reiterated in Leviticus 23:22. It is instructive to note that in this Levitical regulation, the enactment of the law that grants the poor the right to glean rests not on the gleaners, but on the owners of the field who are morally bound to leave the overspill of the harvest, precisely, for gleaning. From this biblical optic, we can see that the businesses Varda encounters on this leg of the journey represent a mockery of this principle. They leave tons of surplus because of over-production and shrewd business practices; not because of a social conscience, but because of a lack of it. They would rather let the food rot than let the poor and hungry glean for their daily bread.

On her next stops, Varda shows us other locations and occasions for gleaning. The camera pans across the sea to Noirmoutier island, which is renowned for its oysters. The shellfish are cultured in oyster beds or cages that are submerged in the inter-tidal zone, that part of the beach where the ebb and flow of the tide becomes most apparent. Here, it is nature that opens a gateway for oyster gleaning—storms cause the oysters to break loose from their cages while the tide washes them ashore. Curiously, it is Christmastime and the farmers are too busy to attend to the lost oysters so that they leave them for the gleaners to collect. Not to over-read theological meaning for this turn of events except to say that nature and religious culture had aligned serendipitously and meaningfully so that an opportunity opens for the gleaners to collect the oysters at such a festive season in the Christian calendar. Yet another encounter with gleaning arises when Varda travels to the urban landscape of Paris. Here, gleaning is done in the trash bins and back alleys of Supermarkets and homes where an assortment of food is regularly dumped because of lapsed expiration dates or because they had fallen short of quality control. Varda meets a group of disaffected youth who dig through supermarket trash bins and got involved in a legal tussle with management, a man who claims he's been subsisting on 100% trash for the last ten years, two trash collectors who have become surrogate family to each other as they feast on expired food. And then she meets a man in his 30s foraging through the piles of trash after a market day. Unlike the gleaners she had previously met, this one is eating discarded food on the spot; the camera captures footage of him eating parsley and other greens directly from the trash. A vegetarian, apples, greens, and bread make up his staple diet. He gleans because he does not earn enough selling street papers and magazines but surprisingly, he claims to have obtained a Master's degree. When Varda follows him further, she discovers that he lives in a shelter that houses a number of immigrants. During evenings, the man offers his neighbors pro bono French lessons. Consistent with the leitmotif of irony that marks Varda's encounters with gleaners, the one who has so little gives so much.

The Gleaners and I is bookended by another painting. As the film comes to a close, Varda visits the museum in Villefranche and requests to view "Gleaners Fleeing before a Storm" (also known as "Gleaners at Chambaudoin"), a 1857 painting by Pierre-Edmond Hédouin. The Hédouin piece looks like a sequel of the Millet painting shown at the film's opening. Here, the gleaners have bundled up their gleanings and head for shelter as a gathering tempest looms in the horizon. The museum staff agrees to bring the painting outdoors for a better view. Varda notes the pleasure of seeing the painting while an actual gale blows against it. Connecting the dots, we can see this as a reflective piece that dramatizes the vulnerability and precariousness of the gleaners' quest for daily bread, and the lack of care and compassion among those who sacrifice their "heart" at the altar of profit. In her own lighthearted, whimsical way, Varda the filmmaker already made this point earlier albeit in eloquent cinematic language—in close-up shots of gleaned surplus potatoes with the peculiar shape of a heart.

DOXOLOGY: EATRIP

Our exploration of the short film *ICHTHUS* brought us to grapple with the ancient question of how a God of bounty and goodness squares with the "meager catch" that people in the margins have to live with in the laborious search for daily bread. The next film *The Gleaners and I* shifts the question and takes it to an anthropological turn as it enters the subterranean world of gleaners who scrounge for food from the discarded surplus of hyper-producing businesses that often remain impassive and uncharitable. The third and final title, the Japanese documentary *Eatrip*, serves as an integrative, doxological piece that tries to find a sense of harmony and gratitude for the blessing that is food, most especially, in its simple, organic forms.

"What is your most memorable meal?" It is curious but not in the least surprising that the answer given by one of the men interviewed in the film, a ballet dancer, was daily bread:

> BALLET DANCER: My mom was a housewife so we ate at home everyday. My dad loved to eat silver-skinned fish so we ate herring, sardines, mackerel, horse mackerel, and scabbard fish, grilled with salt. That was the daily fare for us.

When the other interviewees in the film are asked a similar question, they likewise name daily, staple food. "Rice. Brown rice," a housewife says. "Boiled green peas," exclaims one man. And a grandmother selling vegetables answers, "radish and spinach with sesame." The inspiration for the film *Eatrip* is the idea of simplicity.

"We embark on a journey to explore the meaning of a 'simple life' through the universal act of eating," the voice of filmmaker Yuri Nomura sets the direction for her documentary as we see black and white stills of the group of intriguing personalities—a housewife, a Buddhist monk, a singer, a fashion designer, a tea ceremony master, among others—she will be featuring.

Delectable food preparation scenes proliferate throughout the documentary and we shall mention a couple of them here. Early on in the film, we see the hands of an unidentified person preparing two freshly dressed chickens—they were captured live from a chicken coop in the opening sequence—for cooking. Salt and lemon halves are consecutively rubbed on the chicken. They are then stuffed with the lemon rind and herbs, and then sealed. Later, we discover that the chickens will be submerged in soup stock and seasoned with herbs. There is a freshness and beauty to the simplicity of the food preparation and the same can be said when we see scenes of a large lump of dough being kneaded and sliced for baking, or water being mixed with grain. But before she proceeds with her culinary journey, Nomura first takes a detour and offers a critical look at what is not right with Japanese food culture. She visits Tokyo's famed Tsukiji fish market at the break of dawn and observes how tuna, a prized commodity used for such Japanese staples as sashimi and sushi, and other seafood, are deposited in the market and expertly graded and sold by traders before they find their way to restaurants in Tokyo, and to culinary centers of the world. Mr. Takahashi, a fish wholesaler, explains how seafood is often seasonal and that was respected in the past; people only served fish that were in season. Nowadays, he laments that the Japanese population, most especially around Tokyo, consumes fish all year round regardless of seasonality, evidenced as it were by a decrease in the amount and quality of seafood that land in the market.

Although counter-cultural, *Eatrip* does not dwell on social critique, nor is it interested in adopting a tone of stridency. As the film unfolds, Nomura takes a lyrical and loving glimpse at the lives of people who have gone back to the basics and paid more careful attention to how and what they eat daily. A particularly notable scene is her interaction with Naoko Morioka, a housewife who moved to Okinawa to live in a cabin in the mountains. Wide-angle shots of a natural countryside landscape cues us to the way of life Morioka had chosen for herself and her two young children, which is characterized by self-sufficiency through home gardening, and detachment from modern conveniences such as refrigeration and tap water. She grows and harvests her own vegetables and spices, and draws water from available natural sources. A closer relationship with the earth is the hallmark of this lifestyle. As we see close-up shots of Morioka winnowing tiny edible grains on a woven tray, she marvels at how such a tiny seed grows to become a big plant that produces thousands of seeds, and how privileged she is to take a front row seat to this phenomenon, and, ultimately, to be able to eat the seeds, "To witness these miracles everyday. . . it's mysterious, it's amusing, it makes me happy, it's fun. And it's edible!" Regardless of whether Morioka identifies with a specific faith community, her "para-religious" appreciation of natural food as mysterious and miraculous echoes the theological understanding of the earths' fruits as part of a blessed creation that evinces God's grace and love. In the anthology *The Spirit of Food: 34 Writers on Feasting and Fasting Toward God*, Cincinnati-based pediatrician and gardener Brian Volck shares some meaningful insights that resonate with Morioke's:

> In the garden plants are my teachers. I till, enrich, and water the soil; plant, fertilize, and protect my seedlings; trellis, prune, and harvest my crop, but all my work really amounts to is this: I cooperate with the usual miracles and witness the outward signs of a mysterious, inward grace.[4]

A shared sense of awe and gratitude is the common thread that connects the people featured in the film. They are members of the universal and interdependent eating ecumene, linked for life with Creator, co-creatures, and the created world.

4. Volck, "Late October Tomatoes," 11.

From Eatrip © 2011 New People Entertainment

In its doxological ending, *Eatrip* gathers these personalities to-gether in a tent under a moonlit sky to share a special meal—"a feast of humanness"[5]—they themselves had cooked from natural ingredients. The food preparation scenes, in fact, had all along been lead-ins to the celebration. The camera lingers at the beau-tiful, fresh produce—beans and berries, onions and tomatoes, grains and potatoes—that make their way to form the symphony of ingredients for the savory home-cooked dishes simmering on the stove.

As *Eatrip* proposes, a life lived in simplicity and in commu-nity, coupled with a reverential gratitude for the blessings of the earth, offers some promising, positive, practical prospects in the universal quest for daily bread. A fresh start, if you will. We might think that this recipe is too simple for the complex, consumerist world we live in. But it's a good recipe. Simple, but good.

DAILY BREAD

The conviction that God faithfully offers daily nourishment for be-lievers is well established in the Bible. The desert narrative in Exo-dus 16 represents the faithfulness of Yahweh who provides Israel, sojourning out of Egyptian captivity, with manna in the morning

5. Barbotin, *The Humanity of Man*, 337.

and quail in the evening. Biblical scholar François Bovon notes that the narrative is not simply a statement of God's providence but a theology that is paradigmatic for the life of faith:

> Exodus 16 offers a theology of daily life: believers are on a community trek; the God in whom they place their trust guarantees them what is necessary. The gift is sufficient and is proportionate to each person's needs.[6]

But the prism of the three films we had just explored—*ICHTHUS*, *The Gleaners and I*, and *Eatrip*—brings to light some critical questions on how belief in God's provision of daily bread squares with contemporary realities on the ground where socio-economic forces that are often too large, too complex, to comprehend, bedevil what was intended to be a meaningful and straightforward faith equation. Alluding to the self-same question, Bovon suggests that the root of the problem is the paucity of faith in the part of the human side of the covenant:

> Any lack of confidence, any fear for the morrow that might express itself in excessive acquisition of capital, would lead to a disastrous outcome. . . This theology does not concern isolated individuals or the community taken by itself, as a unit, but rather the interactions between the partners to the covenant. The process of acquisition, distribution, and use of goods do, to be sure, involve "us," but also "you" and "me."[7]

The lack of faith in God's providence results in a deep insecurity about the future, and this drives individuals, groups, nations, and economic systems, to covet and amass the world's goods with little regard for the implications this may have on others.

In the Gospel of Luke (11:3), "Give us each day our daily bread" lies at the heart of Jesus' prayer to the Father. There are varying arguments in scholarship as to what constitutes "daily bread" exactly, but it cannot be denied that in antiquity, most food were prepared and shared on a daily basis and this was true

6. Bovon, *Luke 2*, 88.

7. Ibid.

especially with bread.[8] This dovetails with the perspective of Luke who understands the supplication in a distributive sense, thus, his use of the expression "each day;" the Lukan prayer is an invitation for God to provide daily bread each day in the long view of one's life.[9] Today, the prayer for daily subsistence is as much a vertical prayer directed toward God, as it is a horizontal prayer directed toward the hoarding ecumene that we had become. From the wisdom we had gleaned from our theological engagement with the three films, our daily bread is the marriage of human and divine agency. Foodways and faithways kiss one another. When, in faith, we let go of our close-fisted insecurity, open our hands, and share, then both covenant partners ensure that all members of the human family will receive their daily bread. . . or daily rice, maize, potatoes, beans, yams.

---

8. Yamauchi writes, "In antiquity, much of the food, such as bread, was prepared daily and would be apportioned daily. The daily bread was the very symbol for subsistence, representing the minimal need for existence." Reed, *The Anchor Bible Dictionary*, 779.

9. Bovon, *Luke 2*, 88.

3

Identity Simmers
in the Cooking Pot

The Lunchbox
The Hundred-Foot Journey

"COOKING FROM THE HEART" is a metaphorical expression I often hear when cooks, whether of the home or professional type, draw deep into the pantry of their own personal histories and emotions, and creatively translate what they find into the cooking pot. This is not as deliberate as it sounds, in fact, it may well be second nature for most. It is, after all, a type of cooking that is necessarily wedded with one's very identity. Cultural Identity. National identity. Gender identity. Religious identity. You are what you cook. Or perhaps you cook what you are. The link between cooking and identity is the special interest of this chapter, and the focal point is the rich and ancient food culture of India. Indian cuisine, specifically, food from Mumbai, serves as the central motif in *The Lunchbox* (Ritesh Batra, India, 2013) and *The Hundred-Foot Journey* (Lasse Hallström, U.S., 2014). Although different in a number of ways—

genre, mood, style, country of origin—both films portray Indian food as the medium in and through which identity is discerned, clarified, and reclaimed. In *The Lunchbox*, a critically acclaimed Indian film that received a rousing twelve-minute standing ovation at the 66th Cannes International Film Festival, the legendary Mumbai lunchbox delivery system is the human resource network that nurtures intimacy in a fragile, long-distance relationship between two strangers. Indian food comes mainly in the flavorful packed lunches that the lead female character, a young wife who struggles to recover a sense of her true worth as a woman, prepares for her impassive husband.

Backed by such big name producers as Steven Spielberg and Oprah Winfrey, *The Hundred-Foot Journey* is the filmic re-telling of Richard C. Morais' popular novel of the same title. The whimsical comedy-drama follows the migration of the Kadam family who serendipitously end up in a small village in Southern France where they decide to put up an Indian restaurant. This sets the stage for a gastronomic clash with the Michelin-starred French restaurant just a hundred feet across the street. Conflicted by cultural issues and the lure of success, one of the Kadam sons draws from his Mumbai food memories to re-connect with his cultural identity as a chef.

Through the bold and spicy Indian dishes that flavor the lives of the characters in these two films, theological insight remains subtle and allusive, savory undertones that simmer in the pot, yet making all the difference in providing richness to the final dish that is the cinematic narrative.

A LUNCHBOX CLOSER TO HAPPINESS

Mumbai's legendary lunchbox delivery system can be likened to a precision watch. It functions on the basis of a simple concept, but it requires a sophisticated automaton of moving parts to actually run it. Known as *dabbawala*, literally, "can-carrier," in reference to the stainless tiffin canisters (*dabba*) that stack together in a portable cylinder, the straightforward mission of the lunchbox delivery system is to carry lunchboxes from home kitchens to offices, and then to collect the empty lunchboxes and deliver them back. The process simply re-starts the next day and each of the following days of the working week. The logistics, however, is anything but simple. About 5,000 *dabbawalas* carry some 130,000 lunchboxes a day on foot; and by cart, bicycle, scooter, and railway, under scorching sun and monsoon rain, through Mumbai's urban chaos, to the correct delivery address. On time. Each time. The efficiency of the *dabbawala* delivery system has been the stuff of legend. Stefan Thomke, a Harvard Business School researcher, conducted a study on the system's astonishing service record.[1]

Ironically, the *dabbawala* system's slim probability of committing a service error, not its close-to-perfect precision, serves as the portal through which two lonely souls, Saajan (Irrfan Khan) and Ila (Nimrat Kaur), find a fragile connection in *The Lunchbox*. "Sometimes, the wrong train will get you to the right station," as a memorable line in the film goes.

Ila is an attractive, middle-class housewife who is bound-up in another kind of system, one that relegates her to performing a daily routine of domestic chores that include seeing her small daughter off to school, doing the laundry, going shopping, cooking meals, and preparing lunch for her busy, emotionally distant husband, in time for the *dabbawala* pick-up service. Prompted by an unseen neighbor she calls "Auntie" who often bellows culinary and romantic advice from her upper floor apartment, Ila cooks delectable dishes on the dubious, time-worn assumption that the way to a man's heart is through his stomach. When, uncharacteristically, the lunchbox returns empty again and again, Ila tries to solicit cooking feedback from her husband and gets nothing but cryptic, dismissive replies. She discovers shortly that the *dabbawala* had been delivering to the wrong office address. The widower Saajan Fernandes, an aloof claims clerk nearing retirement after 35 years of bureaucratic service, had been receiving the lunchbox and

1. Thomke, "Mumbai's Model of Service Excellence." For Thomke's reaction to the *The Lunchbox*, which, diegetically, mentions his research, see Shapiro, "A Harvard Study Spices Bollywood Romance in 'The Lunchbox.'"

savoring her cooking. When Ila decides to insert a short note into the lunchbox to inform the then anonymous recipient about the mistake, she receives a reply-note in return, and this soon develops into a regular exchange. What had started as receptive feedback on her cooking becomes a mutual sharing of confidences.

In the meantime, Saajan develops a bond with Shaikh (Nawazuddin Siddiqui), the bright-eyed-and-bushy-tailed employee who was appointed to be his replacement. Previously, he found ways to avoid the gregarious young man who nagged him incessantly for a training session. But when Shaikh, in a moment of vulnerability, confesses to being a self-made orphan, Saajan warms-up to him and eases into becoming a father figure.

Food gets the spotlight early on in *The Lunchbox*. In the film's opening sequence, we see Ila's resolve to prepare a sumptuous lunch for her husband. The camera tells us that this is not lunch packed for gastronomic convenience as in a peanut-butter-and-jelly sandwich; it is a full, four-tiered hot meal (each dish to its own *dabba* canister) consisting of a main curry-based dish, green beans sautéed in chili, steamed rice, and the staple Indian flatbread *naan*. Guided by the voice of her upper floor neighbor Deshpande Auntie or simply "Auntie," who often passes on spices lowered on a basket by the window "dumbwaiter" style, we see Ila's passion and commitment as she prepares each dish.

From The Lunchbox © 2014 Sony Pictures Home Entertainment

The cinematography—close-ups of Ila's hands, assuredly working on the appetizing ingredients—ritualizes her cooking in a manner that is subtly reminiscent of the cooking scenes in the iconic food film *Babette's Feast*. While sharing neither the contemplative gaze, nor the unambiguous religious impulses, of the Danish film, *The Lunchbox* does offer connotations that go deeper than the sheer act of preparing meals. Ila is pouring her heart into her cooking; it is the safe medium through which she can disclose her inner thoughts and feelings. Ila's voice, heard as narration, adds a layer of meaning to the cooking scenes as it reveals the contents of her letters. The personal notes she writes are textual confirmations of what she had already expressed in her food; on the other end, Saajan offers validation by savoring her delicacies, and then writing back. Even Ila's negative emotions find their way into her cooking. When she prepares *paneer kofta* (a mash of Indian cottage cheese, potatoes, and spices, formed into balls, and deep fried), a dish that happens to be her husband's favorite, Saajan writes to let her know that "the food is very salty today." With Auntie's egging, Ila would rebuke his lack of appreciation by sending dishes that are so fiery hot, Saajan needs to douse the fire by eating bananas.

Through food and word, Ila and Saajan find a safe space where they are free to reveal to each other their heartbreaks and their dreams. And through food and word, both of them experience an undeniable transformation. Saajan, who lives in the close-knit Catholic neighborhood of Bandra, and who is presumably a Catholic himself,[2] is initially portrayed as standoffish, reclusive, and quite evidently, lonesome. In a couple of scenes, he is shown looking out the window of his empty house, observing his neighbors as they enjoy the family dinner. Dinners for Saajan have been a solitary affair, nothing more than a forgettable bite in front of the TV. Dining by oneself is the inverse of the Catholic understanding of a meal as a profound, sacramental, table fellowship; implicitly,

2. Although director Ritesh Batra mentions in interviews that the character of Saajan Fernandes is Catholic, there's little outward evidence of this in the film, ". . . he has little connection with those who live next door to him, and has no recognizable trait or quirk of a Catholic man living in a close-knit Bandra neighbourhood." Sharma, "Film Review: *The Lunchbox*," para. 7. I submit that Fernandes's Catholic sensibility comes to play, precisely, by way of his awareness of the impoverishment of his lonely existence.

this is, at the very least, in Saajan's consciousness. He is aware that eating meals in isolation is impoverished indeed.

The deepening mutuality mediated by Ila's lunchbox rekindles the verve in Saajan's life. He begins to notice the simple joys of his day-to-day routine. In one scene, he spots distinct differences in a row of seemingly identical paintings by a street artist, and sees himself in one of the figures portrayed in one of them. In another, he remembers the delicate moments of bliss that he shared with his late wife, small things that he had taken for granted. In yet another instance, he returns a stray ball to the neighborhood kids instead of his usual Scrooge-like practice of confiscation. One kid, a young girl who happens to be a member of the dining family Saajan had observed, waves at him when she sees him by the window; previously the sight of Saajan prompted her to shut the window. And meaningfully, Saajan agrees to stand singularly as "family" for Shaikh during the latter's wedding.

Between the two lead characters, it is Ila who sets out on a more profound transformative journey. Following the rude awakening from her husband's unfaithfulness, a discovery she made when she smells the scent of another woman while doing his laundry, she writes about her dream of moving to neighboring Bhutan, a tiny country that measures its worth in terms of Gross National Happiness (GNH) instead of the normative Gross Domestic Product (GDP). Drawn from an actual holistic philosophical paradigm envisioned and promoted by Bhutan's national leaders, GNH represents a sustainable balance between material and non-material values as an index of its people's well-being. Curiously, Ila is a resident of Mumbai, the Indian city with the highest GDP. Ila's horizon-widening dream bespeaks her simmering dissent against her husband's singular focus on earning a living to the detriment of "non-material values" such as mutuality and faithfulness. The Bhutan piece is a liberative step for Ila considering that she had prologued her letter with an admission of powerlessness over her husband and her marriage, "I thought I should confront him, but I don't have the courage." At once, it is also a positive appeal; Ila articulates her utopian vision of an alternative life, a life authentically lived, where she may re-claim the sense of self that she deserves as a woman.

Reality further crystallizes for Ila when, in an unequivocal lament, her widowed mother (Lilette Dubey) shares her true feelings about being a submissive wife to an autocratic husband. The latter now bedridden, he depends on her personal care-giving and attention 24/7. Unintentionally, she mirrors back to Ila the meaningless redundancy of her servile life:

> ILA'S MOTHER: I'm very hungry. I'm craving *parathas*. I didn't eat breakfast this morning. I was making breakfast for him. I was always worried about what would happen to me when he passed away. But now, I just feel hungry. In the beginning, there was a lot of love between us, when you were born. But the past few years, I've been disgusted by him. Every morning, his breakfast, his medicine, his bath. . . breakfast, medicine, bath. . ."

It is worth noting that Deshpande Auntie, the other significant woman character in Ila's life, shares the plight of her mother; she herself had sacrificed her life to care for a husband who is in a vegetative state. One way or the other, the three women characters in the film appear to have been conditioned to accept as a given the patriarchal ideal of a submissive and long-suffering wife. They are kindred with generations of women elsewhere in the world whose lives reflect similar stories of victimhood, a lot of which is centered on meal preparation. Writer Gina Ochsner relates her own family's sobering version of the story:

> For so many women in my family, the kitchen was a place of thankless repetition, a place where capable women made functional, serviceable food. For my mother, as a young girl living in Prospect, Oregon, the meal needed to have plenty of starches to soak up the whiskey her father, Papa, would likely have consumed on his way home from the power plant. Most importantly, the meal needed to be on the table when he rattled the back door, otherwise, he'd go to the woodpile and drink. . . And so as a young girl, my mother learned that meal preparation

was a preventive act, part of a vast system of damage control, not a nutritive act.[3]

Meal preparation as a "preventive act" is the scarlet thread that
binds Ila and the other women-characters in the film. Beneath the
nobility of putting the needs of their husbands above their own
lies an emotionally and psychologically destructive codependency
that diminishes their sense of identity and human agency. More
than anything, it represents the loss of mutuality. This is especially
descriptive of Ila's situation. At first, Ila's cooking was directed
towards winning back the affections of her husband; here, his
feedback is sacralized as the word of life or death for the state of
their relationship and their marriage. Yet deep inside, Ila knows
there is not much to expect. In one revealing exchange, Deshpande
Auntie tells Ila that her husband will build her a Taj Mahal after
he takes a bite of the delicious meal she had just prepared for him.
Ila's response is pregnant with meaning, "The Taj Mahal is a tomb,
Auntie." Shooting back quickly, the older woman exclaims, "I
know that!"

Noticeably, Ila's earlier dishes are more elaborate, representing her deliberate, even desperate, efforts, to win her husband's approval. Saajan would issue an inadvertent critique of Ila's "damage
control" cooking; when she prepares her husband's favorite dish,
he notes that it is too salty. But as mutual trust grows between Ila
and Saajan, her dishes become less complicated, more flavorfully
balanced. She is no longer cooking for damage control; her food
preparation is restored as a "nutritive act."

Returning to the scene of her mother's confessional, Ila's
wordless reaction is captured in a close-up shot. The expression
etched poetically on the canvass of her face is a threshold to the
deep insight simmering within her. At this unsettling crossroad,
Ila knows that she must cut the scarlet thread of victimhood and
choose a new, life-giving pathway for herself.

There are no clear-cut mentions of theology or religion in *The
Lunchbox*. But having said that, Ila's liberative journey as a woman

---

3. Ochsner, "Filled to Brokenness: Notes to Hunger," 150.

dovetails with feminist theology's quest for women's flourishing. Expressed as a critical principle in Rosemary Radford Ruether's classic work *Sexism and God-Talk*, feminist theology upholds as redemptive whatever promotes the full, authentic humanity of women:

> The critical principle of feminist theology is the promotion of the full humanity of women. Whatever denies, diminishes, or distorts the full humanity of women is, therefore, appraised as not redemptive. . . must be presumed not to reflect the divine, or to reflect the authentic nature of things, or to be the message or work of an authentic redeemer or a community of redemption.[4]

Conversely, Ruether also articulates the critical principle in an affirmative sense– whatever does promote women's flourishing authenticates and affirms the words and actions of a redeemer or a redemptive community as true expressions of the divine. Appropriating this critical principle for Ila's quest for a fuller humanity, the divine presence is construed as kinetic, not static; more a verb than a noun. God is the liberative current sublimated in Ila's silent protest and eventual rejection of the lopsided relationship that relegates her to a derivative existence. At one and the same time, God is the hope-inspiring promise that emboldens Ila to dream of a more meaningful and actualized life. The twin realities of negation and affirmation co-exist in a creative tension. They are two sides of the same coin.

Caught up in the emancipative spirit of her journey, Ila cuts the scarlet thread. With her daughter, she is moving to Bhutan where happiness is a promise and a possibility. The ending of *The Lunchbox* suggests that Saajan may be moving to Bhutan with Ila but as to whether it actually comes to pass remains open-ended. We could only surmise from the genuine mutuality in Sajaan and Ila's relationship, meal after sumptuous meal, that the prospects are good.

4. Rosemary Radford Ruether also configures this critical principle in an affirmative principle, what does promote women's full humanity is deemed redemptive. *Sexism and God-Talk: Toward a Feminist Theology*, 18–19.

COOKING TO MAKE GHOSTS

As in *The Lunchbox*, Indian food figures meaningfully in *The Hundred-Foot Journey*. In flashback, we see the seven-year-old Hassan Kadam (Rohan Chand), the son of restaurant owners, awash in the organized chaos of an open-air food and produce market in Mumbai. His mother (Juhi Chawla) is ushering him into the heart of Indian culinary culture, opening his senses to the tastes, smells, and colors of various ingredients. With his creative mother as his mentor and the family restaurant as his test kitchen, the young Hassan seems destined to become a great chef.

The next time we see Hassan, he is a young man (Manish Dayal) arriving in Saint-Antonin-Noble-Val, a small French village in the South of France. With his migrant family, he has been drifting through Europe and England after political violence in Mumbai had destroyed the restaurant business and killed his mother. Following a chance auto accident and the kindness of a local—a young woman named Marguerite (Charlotte Le Bon)— Papa Kadam (Om Puri) decides to settle in the French village and put up an Indian restaurant he names *Maison Mumbai* ("Mumbai House"). This sets the stage for a clash with the perfectionist Madame Mallory (Helen Mirren), the proprietor of *Le Saule Pleureur* ("The Weeping Willow"), a Michelin-starred French restaurant just a hundred feet across the street. Mortified by the bold spices, bombastic music, and flamboyant Taj Mahal-inspired façade across her classy restaurant, Madame Mallory describes the new establishment as "The death of good taste." She schemes to embarrass Papa Kadam and his restaurant, and he promptly responds in kind. In the crossfire of the gastro-cultural feud, tentative romantic feelings bloom between Hassan, then the head cook of *Maison Mumbai*; and Marguerite, who turns out to be a sous chef at *Le Saule Pleureur*. After loaning Hassan a classic French cookbook, Marguerite tells him that Madame Mallory never interviews job applicants but asks them to make her an omelette, knowing from one bite if they have "it." One evening, some xenophobes attempt to burn down the *Maison Mumbai*, and Madame Mallory discovers that one of her chefs was involved. She fires him immediately and volunteers to scrub the hate messages spray-painted on the perimeter fence of the Indian restaurant. The gesture warms things up a bit between her and Papa Kadam, but things get complicated when Hassan, hands bandaged from burns, asks Madame Mallory to help him cook an omelette. Improvising with Indian flavors from the spice jars he inherited from his mother, Hassan's omelette so impresses Madame Mallory that she waits for him inside the Indian restaurant overnight, determined to hire him as a sous chef. After a heated discussion and a brief haggle over salary with the unyielding Papa Kadam, Madame Mallory succeeds in hiring Hassan. Punctuating classic French dishes with Indian herbs and spices, Hassan's genius helps *Le Saule Pleureur* win a 2-star Michelin rating. Hassan's meteoric rise to fame becomes his ticket to the Paris restaurant scene where he specializes in molecular gastronomy and achieves celebrity chef status. Amid the adulation of critics and foodies, the food memories imparted to him by his late mother never leaves him; he feels a profound longing for the soulful Indian cooking that is his heritage.

There are a couple of food-related themes that stand out in *The Hundred-Foot Journey*. First is the divide between the culinary cultures of India and France. In the film, *Maison Mumbai* represents food as a sensory expression of heritage and home.

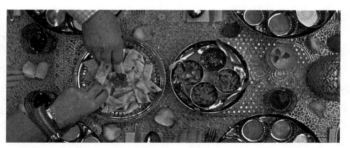

From The Hundred-Foot Journey © 2014 Walt Disney Studios

Food in the Kadam's eatery looks and tastes like Mumbai—lively, versicolored, and audaciously spicy. A regional sampling of the robust, 5,000-year-old national cuisine of India, the Mumbai dishes served by the Kadams are not simply meant to be festive treats for the palate, they are hearty reminders of their roots as a migrant family. Their food is their soul. On the other hand, *Le Saule Pleureur,* drawing from a proud culture that had set culinary standards for the western world since the medieval period, interprets cuisine as edible art and as a tradition of refinement. Like any art form, French cooking is both a matter of gift and consummate skill. Every dish in Madame Mallory's restaurant is an aesthetic delight prepared with surgical precision. Validated by the restaurant's Michelin star, the drive for excellence and perfection is also embodied in Madame Mallory's exacting work ethic. Holding up a limp asparagus, she scolds her chefs with an acerbic reminder: "In this restaurant, the cuisine is not an old, tired marriage, it is a passionate affair!" The contrast between the two culinary cultures is dramatized in the film by way of strategic editing. In the opening night of *Maison Mumbai,* the scene shows the Indian restaurant literally steaming with boisterous food preparation; we see large ladles mixing and scooping South Indian delicacies such as chicken *korma* (literally, "cooked meat," it consists of chicken braised in stock and yogurt, spiced with coriander and cumin). The camera then cuts away to *Le Saule Pleureur* where an exceedingly minimalist dish—vegetable mousse with chanterelle mushrooms—is being prepared with the finesse of an artist's delicate brushstrokes on canvass.

The second theme, the power of food memories to awaken personal and cultural identity, is the one I wish to draw more attention to. The fusion of flavors, textures, colors, and smells from cooking and eating certain foods can plumb into our personal histories and trigger powerful remembrances of people, places and events. Food memories are, essentially, our autobiographical memories.[5] For Hassan, Indian food brings him back to the moments of his childhood when he was receiving precious culinary guidance from his mother. These memories, rendered in flashback

5. For a scientific yet accessible study of food memories as they relate to brain function, see Allen, *The Omnivorous Mind,* 149–185.

scenes of Mumbai, are introduced in the film's prologue. Mama Kadan has taken the boy Hassan with her to the busy market, jostling with buyers to bid on live sea urchins. Unnoticed by all except by the seller, Hassan takes one in his hand and breathes-in the scent of its briny freshness. "To the boy who knows," the seller exclaims, and awards the bid to him. Years later, as a teenager, another flashback shows Hassan observing his mother intently as she stirs a simmering pot of spicy sea urchin stew. "Sea urchins taste of life," she comments. Sea urchin, in fact, is not a protein normally associated with Indian cooking. Director Hallström can be faulted for taking creative license here, putting realism on a level of secondary importance, in favor of using food as a deliberate metaphor. It is arguable whether this stylistic option compromises the authenticity of the film's overall representation of Indian cuisine and its role in cultural memory. But going with the direction of the film, to link the oceany flavor of raw sea urchin with "life" is not at all far-fetched. In an autobiographical piece, novelist Chang Rae-Lee describes a similar childhood encounter with sea urchin roe:

> What does it taste like? I'm not sure, because I've never had anything like it. All I know is that it tastes alive, something alive at the undragged bottom of the sea; it tastes the way flesh would taste if flesh were a mineral.[6]

The full meaning of Mama Kadam's "sea urchins taste of life" analogy is illuminated further when she explains, "To cook, you must kill. You cook to make ghosts, ghosts that live on in every ingredient." As she drips the sauce on the young man's palm for him to sample, she asks, "Can you taste them?"

---

6. Rae-Lee, "Sea Urchin," 441.

From The Hundred-Foot Journey © 2014 Walt Disney Studios

To be sure, the culinary metaphor of "tasting ghosts" in one's food may not be the most appetizing thing to say to a child, but it does describe the death-life dimension in cooking and eating, and, imaginatively, the crucial role that food memories will play in Hassan's identity as a chef. On the level of connotation, the statement is also a foreshadowing of Mama Kadam's violent demise and the way by which her spirit lives on as food memories that will find flavorful expression in Hassan's cooking.

Resonantly, in *The Hundred-Foot Journey*, food memories of Mama Kadam and the culinary legacy she had imparted would be salvific for Hassan; they would play a decisive role in re-rooting Hassan to his cultural identity and restoring soul to his calling as a chef. In the Paris scenes that feature him as a virtuoso chef immersed in the state-of-the-art methods of molecular gastronomy, Hassan finds himself in a lonely space. He is a successful young man with a conflicted inner life. The camera captures him distracted and lost in thought even when he obliges a fan's request for a photo opportunity. There is a void that neither success nor renown can fill. After a long night at work, he chances upon a food porter, an Indian like himself, eating a late dinner. The porter reveals that the dinner is food his wife cooked and packed for him. "Every bite takes you home," he adds. When Hassan obliges an offer to sample some of the food, it kindles a deep emotional response in him. His eyes welling up, Hassan is moved by the home-cooked Indian meal. He is tasting the ghosts that live on in his food memories.

As a culinary artist, Hassan's innermost longing is to be able to offer his very best in his cooking. In order for him to do this, he needs to plumb deep within his Indian soul. In the film *Babette's Feast*, the story of a culinary genius who had been denied the chance to practice her art for many agonizing years, this heartcry is understood to be the prayer of every true artist: "Throughout the world, there goes one long cry from the heart of the artist. Give me leave to do my utmost." Although *The Hundred-Foot Journey* does not share the overtly religious milieu of *Babette's Feast*, it convincingly affirms the transcendence of art when it is created from the clay of authenticity and true inspiration. *The Hundred-Foot Journey* sees the art of cooking as a spiritual act.

The traces of transcendence in Hassan's cooking are symbolically represented by the Indian flourishes that enliven his fusion cuisine. This is already dramatized in the earlier scene when he and Madame Mallory team-up to cook his own intercultural version of the omelette. The blending of ingredients, with a special close-up on the Indian spices scooped out from the spice box Hassan inherited from his mother, highlights the life-giving possibilities of the both-and. Stylistically, the montage unfolds in poetic slow motion, deliberately infusing it with a transcendent mood. An omelette, one of the most deceptively simple dishes to cook, is transformed into a sublime work of edible art. The image-and-music in the omelette scene of *The Hundred-Foot Journey* recalls a sliver from a W. H. Auden poem that appears in the *New Yorker* article entitled "On installing an American Kitchen in Lower Austria." First mentioning an artist-cook having the ability to move people beyond the capabilities of great artists such as Mozart, Auden draws a connection between the sacramental sensibility of a Christian and the eating of a perfectly cooked omelette, the cooking of which, in the latter's opinion, was "a Christian deed."[7] At the end of the sequence, Madame Mallory samples the omelette and is moved to ecstasy. Tellingly, the transcendent quality of Hassan's omelette has much to do with the authenticity of the recipe; it is an omelette cooked with an Indian soul. As British cookery writer Elizabeth

7. Auden, "On Installing an American Kitchen in Lower Austria," 34.

David discerningly affirms, ". . .there is only one infallible recipe for the perfect omelette: your own."[8]

Later, when Hassan seasons the traditional French recipe *Boeuf Bourguignon* ("Beef Burgundy") with the typical Indian spices cumin and mustard seed, Madame Mallory acquiesces and christens the fusion dish "*Boeuf Bourguignon* a la Hassan." In the end, the re-valuing of soulful cooking becomes decisive when Hassan leaves Paris and brings his culinary practice back to Saint-Antonin-Noble-Val. The small village, once a turbulent pot where cultural stereotypes come to a boil, had become a creative space— the marriage of Indian and French culinary cultures. Hassan has come home.

GOD WALKS AMONG THE POTS AND PANS

As we have seen in both the *The Lunchbox* and *The Hundred-Foot Journey*, cooking is not simply about the preparation of food. Upon thoughtful reflection, it represents the discernment of the truths and the untruths about one's identity.

A woman's quest for full humanity in a loveless, unequal marriage, is the consequential theme dramatized in *The Lunchbox*. In the film, an invisible barrier demarcates the kitchen as Ila's ap- pointed space. Not once do we see her husband get close to the kitchen area, let alone cross its artificial fence line. Ila's kitchen symbolizes her derivative existence where her very self-worth is determined by her husband's approval. It is not her cooking that is at stake here, she is. Noted Indian feminist Sarojini Sahoo de- scribes the politics of gender in the Indian home in similar terms. The home kitchen is the wife's fated domain regardless of whether she has taken on a paying job or not. No such expectation is as- cribed to the husband: "A woman has to take charge of the kitchen, even if she is a wage-earning member of the household and holds down a job outside of the home. . . a man who cooks for his family violates the laws of manhood."[9]

8. Elizabeth David as quoted in Brook, *Kitchen Wit*, 55.

9. Lowen, "Feminism in India," para. 13.

In *The Women in God's Kitchen*, a feminist literary analysis of the food metaphors in the spiritual writings of Christian "holy women," Cristina Mazzoni takes note of the historical fact that the home kitchen has not been the best place to find human flourishing, most especially for women:

> Kitchens are humble places. . . Most kitchen work is monotonous, tedious, even, much of it goes unappreciated. . . It is true that, with their changing shape and evolving functions, kitchens have participated in the history of the family, of women, of social classes, and of entire cultures. But women have fought long battles to get out of the kitchen, and what began as a figure of speech, with the kitchen standing for patriarchal oppression, people cook less and less at home in the West. . .[10]

Notwithstanding the stigma associated with the home kitchen, it is through the activity of cooking that Ila experiences moments of redemption and transformation—brushes with the freeing presence of the Divine, if you will—where she is again able to find her voice, express her truth, and re-discover mutuality in her life. Food preparation is renewed as a nutritive act; cooking becomes an endeavor that is both creative and self-creating. As a woman, she is not, by any means, alone in finding "God" in the desert that is the kitchen. Transcending the sentence of their androcentric and patriarchal contexts, the religious women who are the protagonists in Mazzoni's book—Hildegard of Bingen, Sor Juana Inés de la Cruz, and Elizabeth Seton, to mention a few—draw culinary wisdom from the kitchen to describe their encounters with the sacred. One of the most vivid kitchen metaphors described in the book is a piece written by the 16th century Catholic saint Teresa of Avila. In her account of the founding of her convents, posthumously published in 1610 as *The Book of the Foundations*, the Spanish mystic and reformer writes: *Entre los pucheros anda el Señor*—"The Lord walks among the pots and pans."[11] The narrative remembrance of Teresa of Avila who found divine impulses in *lo cotidiano*, the

10. Mazzoni, *The Women in God's Kitchen*, 1.

11. Ibid., 118.

day-to-day rhythms of ordinary chores such as cooking, offer meaningful resonances for contemporary women who have taken on the demands of providing nourishment for their families day by day. Like Ila in *The Lunchbox*, they struggle to stand in the fullness of the truth of who they are: co-equal bearers of full, authentic humanity.

As the quest for authentic gender identity is served as a salient theme in *The Lunchbox*, so is the quest to re-discover cultural identity in *The Hundred-Foot Journey*. As an immigrant from India, cultural identity had become a more liquid concept for the young chef Hassan. Cultural identity lies in the fissure between his Indian cultural heritage and the "host" culture he now swims in, which is French. This is compounded by the creative and commercial demands placed upon him as a culinary *wunderkind*, the tidal force of which pulls him even farther away from "home."[12] For Hassan, the redemptive impulse comes in the form of food memories drawn from his childhood in Mumbai. To recall, a flashback scene reveals his mother's culinary wisdom, a veiled presentiment of her own tragic death and her continued presence in Hassan's cooking: "You cook to make ghosts, ghosts that live on in every ingredient."

The film's quasi-religious treatment of the conjoined themes of death, memory, and new life, draws a soft-focus connection with the memorial character of the Christian eucharist. The Greek word *anamnesis* ("remembrance") appears in Luke's account of Jesus' last supper. "Do this in remembrance of me" (Luke 22:19), he instructs his disciples, as he shares the bread and the wine with them on the eve of his impending death. The continuing fulfillment of this

---

12. In contrast to Ila's home kitchen, Hassan's is a professional kitchen, a domain colonized by male chefs. A detailed analysis of gender inequality in restaurant kitchens is beyond the recipe of this book. Suffice it to say that although women are starting to make inroads in the profession, the maleness of the culinary profession continues to be a prevalent issue. "Hand-wringing about the low status and low numbers of women in the culinary world has been constant since professional cooking changed from a menial trade to a respectable career, beginning in the 1980s." Moskin, "A Change in the Kitchen," para. 21.

message is seen in the post-resurrection accounts of the breaking of the bread (e.g., in Luke-Acts), as well as in Christian liturgical celebrations of the eucharist. It is not just a matter of recalling an event that had transpired in the past, it is a call to witness Christ's transformative presence in the meal. Remembrance of the enduring significance of Jesus as salvation-in-person has profound bearing on the believing community's sense of identity and purpose.

It is, of course, necessary to point out that the representation of food and meals in the *The Hundred-Foot Journey* was never intended to capture the full force of meaning of the Christian eucharist. But the manner by which food memories blend Hassan's past and present into a flavorful meal that nourishes his identity, and infuses a new purpose for his future, are eucharistic flourishes that have as much impact on the story as the inspirited chef's *massala* of heirloom spices that transforms time-worn recipes into culinary miracles.

4

Feasting at the Table
of Finitude

A Simple Life
Departures

IN WHAT MAY SEEM like an incongruous pairing, the relationship between food and death is this chapter's focus of attention. Food, of course, connotes the nourishment and sustenance of life, while death is the decisive expression of human finitude, the end of life. What then is the role of food and eating in the human pilgrimage of life that, ultimately, leads one to face the inescapable reality of death? The two films spotlighted in this chapter come from two of the world's renowned culinary centers, namely, Hong Kong, the "world's food fair" with its mind-boggling variety of gastronomic options front-lined by its famous Cantonese cuisine; and Japan, a country obsessed with the freshness of its food and the art of its unique culinary traditions. It comes as no surprise then that in these cinematic works, food and eating are constitutive elements of the narrative.

Set in contemporary Hong Kong, *A Simple Life* (Ann Hui, 2011) is based on the true story of film producer Roger Lee and his family's servant Chung Chun-Tao, whose life of dedicated servitude ended only when the health challenges of old age physically prevented her from continuing her work. In the film, filmmaker Hui creates a deliberately paced ode to the elderly and, synchronously, quietly observes the importance of foodways in sustaining intergenerational communication and mutuality. Across genres, the transition into the twilight years of a person's life has been a recurring thematic concern in Hui's films, most notably, in *Summer Snow* (1995), *July Rhapsody* (2001), and *The Postmodern Life of my Aunt* (2006), but *A Simple Life* is arguably her most accomplished film. Among its numerous honors are five awards from the 2011 Venice Film Festival.

The Japanese film *Departures* (Takita Yôjirô, 2008) follows the exploits of a man who reluctantly accepts a job that involves administering traditional funeral rites on human remains, an occupation weighted by social stigma in Japan. Food and eating mark the entire cinematic narrative at delicate turns, disclosing their meaningful place in the cycle of life and death that is a given in the human journey. A unique story sensitively and lyrically told, *Departures* won the highly competitive Oscar Best Foreign Language Film Award, besting the early favorite *Waltz with Bashir* (Ari Folman, Israel, 2008), and earning the applause of a global audience. On the same year, it all but swept the awards of the Japanese Academy, winning ten of its thirteen nominations.

A SIMPLE RECIPE

In an early scene in *A Simple Life*, vendors at a Hong Kong food market lightheartedly anticipate the arrival of a special customer. "She's coming," one of them exclaims, trading clued-in glances with the others. An elderly lady, lugging a basketful of vegetables on one hand and a clear plastic bag containing live fish on the other, arrives with a smile on her face. They welcome her cordially and ask her what she needs today. "Garlic," she responds. Donning a coat and putting on a pair of prescription eyeglasses, she makes her way into the walk-in refrigerator and begins to sort through peeled cloves of garlic. With the fussy resolve of a Michelin-starred chef, she picks out the best pieces and puts them into a small bag. To be sure, the fastidious shopper is no professional chef. She is a Hong Kong amah, a stay-home domestic helper named Ah Tao (Deannie Ip), who has been in the service of a Chinese family for more than sixty years. We know from the film's prologue that today, she only serves Roger (Andy Lau), a middle-aged bachelor who opted not to migrate to the United States with the rest of the family.

A special, multi-course seafood lunch awaits Roger at the dining table but his stoic expression suggests that this for him is daily fare.

From A Simple Life © 2013 Well Go USA

Robotically, he puts out his hand, and Ah Tao immediately serves him a bowl of rice. Although he offers Ah Tao neither affirmation nor simple thanks for her effort, the way by which Roger wolfs down the food says it all—the meal is delicious. When lunch is over, Roger parks himself on the living room couch and Ah Tao serves him dessert to go with his cup of tea. Before he takes off posthaste for Beijing where he is working on a film project as a producer, the only words Roger leaves Ah Tao are "It's been ages since I've had ox-tongue."

The predictable rhythm of life is disrupted when, upon returning from Beijing, Roger discovers Ah Tao unconscious after having suffered a serious stroke. Not wanting to be a burden, she insists on moving into an assisted-living home for the elderly. Roger finds suitable accommodations for her in the commercial district of Sham Shui Po in Northwestern Kowloon and, despite Ah Tao's objection, decides to foot the bill. With the bare interiors of the facility, the crowded communal living situation, and housemates who embody the telltale signs of advancing age and imminent death, Ah Tao's first few days in the nursing home is a depressing experience. In a dinner scene, an uninspired meal of dull-looking meat and boiled rice, apportioned on a hospital food tray, is set before her. This is a conspicuous, if not a disheartening, downgrade from the exquisite dishes she prepares for Roger. It doesn't help that she is dining with residents who are in various stages of dementia. Nonetheless, Ah Tao gradually warms up to her new home as she develops meaningful relationships with co-residents and with the staff. She finds a new sense purpose, becoming a thoughtful friend and guileless peacemaker to her housemates as they deal with the unforgiving realities that define their lives. For Roger, the tragedy that had befallen Ah Tao is a reality check; it makes him realize the amah's significant place in his life that goes back to his infancy, and the impending void of her absence. Roger's sensitive side, often belied by his apparent self-absorption and his impassive veneer, begins to shine through, incrementally, but genuinely. Visiting her regularly as her "godson," he spends time in conversation with her, and takes her to restaurant meals. In the simple cadence of their routine, the two find a renewed companionship, one that allows for greater warmth and humanity as Ah Tao faces the inevitable fact of her mortality.

In *A Simple Life*, filmmaker Ann Hui resists the tried-and-tested conventions of a Hollywood melodrama; no copious tears shed on cue, no sentimental embraces, no deathless lines. Instead, deep emotions are calibrated so that they are expressed in small, meaningful gestures. In one playful scene, Ah Tao and Roger behave like teenagers, teasing each other about their old crushes. In another scene, they rummage through Ah Tao's collection of keepsakes, fondly sharing remembrances of their many years together. The on-point performances of the lead actors infuse the characters with a natural authenticity. Deanie Ip, a glamorous character actress who is at least fifteen years younger than her character, embodies Ah Tao with such uncanny realism, it gives the film a documentary feel. She deservingly won acting honors, among them, the Volpi Cup, top acting prize at the 2012 Venice International Film Festival. Andy Lau, an Asian pop megastar, also offers a credible performance; his Roger is an enigma, at once sensitive and unsentimental. Ip and Lau have played mother and son in films for some thirty years, their effortless onscreen chemistry does wonders in making the relationship of Ah Tao and Roger thoroughly convincing.

While praising the film, some critics, including Roger Ebert, found it wanting of a more overt emotional payoff. Such an expectation is misplaced. In *A Simple Life,* Hui clearly premises her lead characters' relationship on understatement; precisely, a quiet dignity sublimates emotions into something more heartfelt and less literal. In a review published in *Time Out Hong Kong,* Edmund Lee affirms Hui's stylistic option: "Potentially a very heavy drama on a person's slow waltz towards death, Hui's realist portrait has benefitted from its determination against the kind of tear-jerking manipulation ubiquitous in similar movies."[1] Similarly, Tara Brady of the *The Irish Times* asserts, "Her milieu is too contemplative and understanding to allow *A Simple Life* to play as outright tragedy or as a showboating tearjerker."[2] Put another way, to expect Hui's delicate portraiture of the personal to crescendo into a flagrant confessional is basically saying that it is not *A Simple Life* that one wishes to see but *Terms of Endearment* (James L. Brooks, USA, 1983). Yet for all its emotional restraint, I submit that a closer observation of the way food and eating figure in the dramatic arc of *A Simple Life* reveals a deep emotional core. Curiously, critics were oblivious to the role of food as an expressive medium between Roger and Ah Tao notwithstanding that it is a lucid and recurring motif in the film's mise-en-scène. Between the two leads,

1. Lee, "A Simple Life," para. 3.
2. Brady, "A Simple Life/*Tao Jie*," para. 5.

emotions are shared not so much by the spoken word or direct action, but through the edible grammar of food. And importantly, it is through shared meals that Ah Tao and Roger find mutual solace and meaning amid the uncertainty and agony that mark the passage from life to death. From the early sequences, we see the earnest effort Ah Tao pours into the meals she prepares for Roger. Only choice ingredients such as live seafood and fresh produce find their way into the dining table, even for everyday fare. We get a fuller sense of the extent of Ah Tao's dedication in an amusing scene when she interviews a few applicants for the job she had just vacated. Her perfectionist's to-do list, a litany of culinary specifications to ensure that her successor will get all the i's dotted and the t's crossed, are enough to drive each one away in utter disbelief or sheer contempt:

> AH TAO: How do you cook your rice? Better to use a clay pot, Miss. . . Do you know where to buy live fish, especially yellow croakers? My master only eats fresh steamed sea fish. When he's home, make him slow-boiled soups. And every second day, cook abalone or sea cucumbers.

For Ah Tao, ordinary meals are occasions to serve lavish dishes. Roger deserves nothing less. We are inclined to think that the special treatment is coming not simply from sheer dedication and a sense of duty but from maternal care and an earnest generosity. Her interaction with Roger offers further validation. When Roger requests that she cook ox-tongue for him, Ah Tao scolds him:

> AH TAO: You want more angioplasty, ha? Forget about it! You had crab today, you shouldn't eat ox-tongue.

As if hearing nothing, Roger shoots back, "I want it stewed." This only elicits a dismissive silence from Ah Tao, but subsequently, her actual response says otherwise. In a series of close-ups, the camera focuses on the wok as Ah Tao sautés garlic and ginger, pours-in hot broth, and adds scallions, star anise, and other spices. She then takes a hefty piece of protein and carefully drops it into the simmering mixture. It is a whole slab of ox tongue. Like a mother who, at times, sets aside rules to allow her son to live a little, Ah Tao has bent backwards to indulge Roger's request. The symbolic equation is clear: Ah Tao's maternal affection for Roger finds physical vocabulary in the food she cooks for him. In this regard, Ah Tao is kindred with the central characters of earlier Asian food films, namely, Mui, the serenely beautiful cook-housekeeper in *The Scent of Green Papaya* (Tranh Anh Hung, Vietnam/France, 1993), whose attraction for her employer is the unseen ingredient that inspires her cooking; and Chef Chu, the patriarch in *Eat Drink Man Woman* (Ang Lee, Taiwan, 1994), who conveys his love for his daughters through the exquisite gourmet dinners he prepares for them each week. In all three films, food is not merely the medium of physiological nutrition, it is the very medium of human relationality. In *A Simple Life*, the deeper meaning attached to food could only mean that Ah Tao's stroke short circuits not just her ability to cook, but the very means by which she is able to communicate her affection to Roger. Given that, the meaningful role of food in their relationship is not completely diminished. Roger would come to a greater appreciation of Ah Tao's devoted care when it is discontinued; he realizes what he is missing. The last dish Ah Tao cooked will help Roger remember. When his old classmates hang out in his flat, one of them raids the fridge and discovers the uneaten stewed ox tongue Ah Tao had earlier prepared. As Roger and his buddies savor the dish, it rekindles fond memories of the *amah* who was a mother figure to all of them. On the other end, Ah Tao's mahjong game with her co-residents is interrupted by a phone call from her "godson;" she is delighted to hear Roger's friends reciting in chorus a silly, familiar poem from their youth. Letting her know how much they miss her, they take turns naming the mouthwatering dishes she had cooked for them—stuffed duck, taro cake, steamed crab, marinated chicken, beef brisket. Not surprisingly, their recollection of Ah Tao comes in the delicious servings of food memories. In his book *The Omnivorous Mind: Our Evolving Relationship with Food*, research scientist John S. Allen notes that the multisensory experience of eating food awakens memories that go further than the gastronomic:

The taste, smell, and texture of food can be extraordi-
narily evocative, bringing back memories not just of
eating the food itself but also of the place and setting
in which the food was consumed. Beyond memories of
taste and place, food is effective as a trigger of even deeper memories of feelings and emotions, internal states of
the mind and body.[3]

Food has always been Ah Tao's way of expressing maternal care,
and even the personalities that form the concentric circles of
Roger's life have been gracious recipients of it. Meaningfully, it is
the stewed ox-tongue, the cooked-to-order dish she prepared in
doting aquiescence to Roger's request, that triggers memories of
her nurturing presence.

As a filial response to the sudden termination of Ah Tao's culinary mothering, Roger takes the latter out on lunch dates at near-
by eateries. Notably, a reversal of roles transpires. Roger is gently
assisting Ah Tao, still recovering from the effects of the stroke, as
she hobbles with him to the restaurant. When they get there, he
orders only one bowl of rice to go with the main course of steamed
fish, claiming that he is always overfed during office meetings. The
underlying reason for this is more noble: Roger wants to help Ah
Tao, who has yet to regain use of her left arm, eat lunch. He cuts
the fish into manageable pieces so she is able to pick them up with
her chopsticks. Unlike Roger's deadpan reaction to the sumptuous
meals she prepared and served him over the years, Ah Tao thanks
him for his kind gesture, not just once, but twice, over a meal he
did not himself cook. She appreciates Roger's effort to express care
and affection, a marked change from his normally ungracious and
disinterested attitude. Here, food and eating take on a deeper significance as signs of mutuality and true conversation earn a place
at the table. As if issuing a corrective to the years of apathy, Roger
would find an opportunity to verbalize his appreciation for Ah Tao
in some token way. Following the amah's verdict that the fish is
good but the sauce is "too salty," Roger jovially comments, "You
were always so fussy, you spoiled the rest of us."

3. Allen, *The Omnivorous Mind*, 150.

Even as the act of eating becomes compromised when Ah Tao's health begins to take a serious downslide, the grammar of food would continue to mark her protracted journey toward death. At a later juncture, Ah Tao is rushed to the hospital because her bile duct is inflamed. This turn of events is consequential: the bile duct is an essential organ of the digestive system. For a life lived around food and cooking, the incongruity is salt to a wound. In this regard, Ah Tao is kindred with Chef Chu, the protagonist in the previously mentioned film *Eat Drink Man Woman*. Acclaimed as Taiwan's greatest culinary genius, Chef Chu loses the bodily sense most proximate to the practice of his art—his sense of taste. This would have implications both for his cooking, and for his relationship with his daughters. Yet, in *A Simple Life*, food would find renewed expression at the very point of the narrative when there is an unambiguous reference to faith. In the film's most overt religious moment, Ah Tao, here, lying on a hospitable bed while Roger and a Bible-bearing pastor stand by her bedside, takes the former's hand and exclaims, "I am not scared, they can do whatever they want." Then turning to the pastor, she asks, "God will arrange things, right?" He replies with the famous passage from the book of Ecclesiastes, "For everything, there is a season, a time for tears and a time for laughter, a time for birth and a time for death. . ." Then in a humorously graced moment, Roger teases, "A time for surgery and bile duct dissection." Half-grimacing in pain between fits of laughter, Ah Tao quickly interjects, "A time for steaming melons, and a time for salted eggs." Cooking remains a constant in the tension between life and death that now threatens her capacity to ingest food; it seethes through in the form of declarative memory, that is, a memory of an event that can be consciously recalled and articulated. On another level, cooking also figures allusively in a religious sense. Mixing the ingredients of assured faith and inescapable mortality, Ah Tao had, in a manner of speaking, cooked a paradox.

Prior to Ah Tao's impending death, we see Roger pushing her on a wheelchair at a park, so she can get some sun. She looks considerably worse than before; her body shaking in tremors, her speech, cryptic. As Roger wipes her mouth with some tissue, Ah Tao repeatedly utters a request. "I want some roast goose. . . roast goose," she says, "roast goose rice noodles." When Roger walks back to Ah Tao's wheelchair after taking a few seconds to throw the tissue into a garbage can, the scene cuts away to the driveway of the nursing home where an unconscious Ah Tao is being wheeled into a waiting ambulance, connoting that she is close to expiring. The editing strategy employed by filmmaker Ann Hui is subtle and poetic, and notably, it also brings the leitmotif of food all the way down to the character's very last breath. In the Japanese food film *Tampopo*, a frail-looking young mother who is at the threshold of death is prodded by her husband to prepare a meal for the family, a desperate attempt to shake her out of her stupor and rekindle her will to live. As if operating on autopilot, the mother gets up, cooks and serves a meal of fried rice, and smiles upon seeing that her husband and kids are eating well. And then, like a candle snuffed out by the wind, she collapses and dies. *A Simple Life* takes it even further. In the film's affecting denouement, Hui uses magic realism to grant us visual access to the transcendence of Ah Tao's devotion toward Roger. From a low angle, the camera shows Ah Tao alive, peering from the window of Roger's upper floor apartment. She quickly shuts off the lights when Roger approaches the building, but he does take pause to gaze at the window as if sensing her presence. As Roger enters the apartment, we see Ah Tao pressing her ear against the kitchen door, listening affectionately to his movements. Beyond death, Ah Tao's care for Roger lives on, and her abiding presence is spatialized by the one area in the house that best represents her maternal devotion: the kitchen.

MAIN COURSE: LIFEDEATH

Coffinman: The Journal of a Buddhist Mortician, the memoir of author Shinmon Aoki, was one of the inspirations for the film *Departures*. A real life *nōkanfu*[4] or "encoffiner," Aoki is a professional

4. According to Yoshiko Okuyama, the Japanese word *nōkanfu* (*nōkan* referring to the act of laying the deceased into a coffin; *fu*, an older term for

hired to perform a traditional Japanese funeral ritual involving the attentive and respectful cleaning, robing, and grooming of the bodies of the departed. To work as an encoffiner is not the most attractive job option for the reason that traditional Japanese culture views corpses as ritually unclean, not to mention that most people in modern Japan die in hospital settings, consequently, making encoffinment superfluous, if not obsolete. From the lens of Buddhist spirituality, Aoki recalls his colorful, poetic, and, at times repugnant, experiences as an encoffiner, coming into contact with the edge of the porous curtain between life and death, and finding signs of hope and beauty in the unexpected. The thematic connections between the book and the film consist of bare allusions rather than a categorical interfacing, but it is noteworthy that the food motif is found solely in the latter; food and eating do not figure in Aoki's memoir. Yet, in the supplemental video interview accompanying the DVD release of *Departures*, filmmaker Takita Yōjirō reveals that the professional encoffiners he has had conversations with validate the purposeful role of food in their work lives:

> TAKITA: I think to live is to eat. The work of an encoffiner is a very difficult job, a difficult task. And when we first saw professional encoffiners at work for research purposes, we saw what they do and asked them, "How do you feel after you perform one of these rituals?" And the first thing they said is, "We just feel hungry. We immediately eat afterwards."

In *Departures*, the encoffiners' shared experience of hunger immediately following an encoffinment translates cinematically into the trope of food that punctuates the cycle of life and death in the narrative. This drapes a meaningful new layer to a story whose central theme is not food and eating but death and dying. There is good reason then to allow *Departures* to speak primarily on its own terms—film *qua* film—and with a considerable degree of autonomy from its literary source material.

---

a man of employable age) was coined by the bereaved families who sought Aoki's services. "Shinto and Buddhist Metaphors in *Departures*," 4–5.

The story of *Departures* revolves around a protagonist who, by some intriguing twist of faith, becomes an encoffiner. Kobayashi Daigo (Motoki Masahiro), a cellist by profession, loses his job when the Tokyo-based orchestra he plays for is disbanded. Disheartened by his sudden joblessness, he is also concerned about his inability to pay for the prohibitive cost of his recently acquired top-of-the-line cello. In light of this unfortunate turn, he and his wife Mika (Hirosue Ryôko) agree to start life anew in his hometown, the idyllic, mountainous prefecture of Yamagata, where his late mother left the small coffee shop she used to operate. Daigo's first priority is to find a new job and, soon enough, he spots an opening through a newspaper ad for an "NK agent." With a vague reference to "assisting departures," he presumes that the job opening is for a travel agent, only to be appalled by the discovery that the firm is involved in *nôkan* or encoffinment; the "NK" standing for *nôkanfu*. With some prodding from proprietor Sasaki Ikuei (Yamazaki Tsutomu) who pays him a generous advance on the spot, Daigo accepts the offer. Because of the stigma and shame attached to being an encoffiner, he keeps his new job a well-guarded secret even from the clueless Mika who thinks he is an events planner of sorts. On his first assignment, Daigo's senses are assaulted by the sight and smell of a maggot-infested corpse in an advance stage of decomposition. The encoffiner-in-training is left badly shaken by this macabre encounter, and he rushes to find some relief in the steaming waters of a public bath, and the warm touch of his wife. But Daigo gradually comes to an acceptance of what he does when he begins to understand the true value of the ritual of encoffinment, not to mention the gratitude of one bereaved family after another. Food, whether home cooked meals he shares with Mika, or servings of fried chicken he shares with his two colleagues in the office, help sustain him through the journey. Daigo's growing appreciation for his occupation would face a rude awakening when whisperings in the village lead to social ostracism, compounded by Mika's discovery of a *nôkanfu* training DVD he was made to do earlier. He comes home one day to a visibly upset Mika who presses the playback button to reveal a scene featuring a naked Daigo acting as a stand-in for a corpse. When he could not give a straight answer to Mika's demand that he resign, she leaves him and moves to her parents' house in Tokyo. After a few months, a now pregnant Mika returns and asks Daigo to find a "respectable" job for the sake of their child, but before he could give an answer, he receives a phone-in assignment for the encoffining of a long-time family friend, the elderly lady who runs the public bath. In the presence of Mika and members of the grieving family, one of whom ostracized him earlier, Daigo performs the ritual with such dignity and artistry that he earns the respect of everyone, including his wife, who realizes the nobility of his work. In the film's ending, Daigo finds himself having to perform the encoffinment of his own father who had been estranged from him since his boyhood. Festering with old wounds of abandonment, Daigo had kept a rock given to him by his father, a "letter-stone" whose texture is said to symbolize what one truly feels. At first, he is unable to see any familiarity with the face of his father, failing to even remember what he truly looked like. But when he unclenches the closed fist of the corpse, he releases a small white stone, the same one he had given to his father when he was a child. As he continues the encoffinment ritual, Daigo begins to recognize the face of the father he once knew.

A harmonious orchestration of poetic imagery, beautiful music, unpretentious acting, and a storyline that touches on the universal human journey toward mortality, *Departures* drew a generally positive reception from critics, with a few negative reactions to the perceived sentimentality and raw display of emotions in the film's funeral scenes. Unlike the subtle emotional undercurrents of *A Simple Life*, *Departures* wears its heart on its sleeve. Ironically, studies appear to validate that Japan is not known to be a country of criers. In a research poll among 37 countries, the International Study of Adult Crying found that the Japanese rank among the least likely to cry,[5] and this seems to be a widely held impression assumed by those unfamiliar with the culture. According to Alex Agran of Arrow Films, a small company that eventually acquired

5. St. Michel, "Crying it Out in Japan," para. 5.

video distribution rights for *Departures* in Britain, this might have played out in the minds of British distributors who were not too keen on picking up the film: "*Departures* is very emotional; it doesn't conform to what people expect from Japanese films."[6]

To be sure, attitudes toward death and grief are shaped to a large extent by cultural values, the web of significance one is born and raised in. Without meaning to homogenize Japanese culture, one key to understanding the representation of emotions in *Departures* is to consider the Japanese communitarian value of "harmony" that is brought to bear in emotional expressions of grief and mourning:

> There is no equivalent to the term *grief* in some other languages; indeed, in some cultures, as in Japan, the concept of emotions that are only in the individual seems foreign. For the Japanese, individual identity is a function of social harmony. Emotions are part of family or community membership, sensed among the members so as to create a harmonized atmosphere.[7]

The notion that emotions are connected with the value of social harmony says a lot about the representation of communitarian mourning in *Departures*. The encoffinment rite offers a harmonized atmosphere to support bereaved families and friends who are only beginning to come to terms with the pain of their loss. It is the safe space to express emotions. "Therefore, the journey to the afterlife is not simply a metaphor of faith, but a coping mechanism within the culture for the very basic and human expression of grieving."[8]

At least in regard to the way *Departures* represents Japanese funerals as the proper venue for overt emotional expression, my own Filipino culture, which is strongly affective and communitarian, is kindred with Japanese culture. But it wasn't until I was exposed to a funeral rite different from what I was used to that

6. Gritten, "*Departures* is not what people expect from Japanese cinema," para. 5.

7. Klass, "Grief and Mourning in Cross-Cultural Perspective," para. 4.

8. Okuyama, "Shinto and Buddhist Metaphors in *Departures*," 17.

I came to clarify this for myself, albeit by way of negation. Some years ago, I attended the funeral mass for a Catholic priest of German descent in an agrarian town in the US Midwest. The first thing I noted was the near absence of emotional expression among the bereaved. Having been raised in a cultural milieu that puts a high premium on emotional intelligence, where the tears the community sheds for a departed member are directly proportional to its love and affection for him or her, it was a bit of a culture shock for me to witness a funeral bereft of tears.[9] The expression and acceptability of emotions in the face of loss is culture specific. People do not simply mourn, they mourn "as."

Be that as it may, I draw attention to our principal focus of exploring the significance of foodways in the cyclic life-death rhythm portrayed in *Departures*. A thematic and stylistic constant, food scenes appear at regular intervals—I counted a total of ten scenes that have to do with food and eating—throughout the cinematic narrative.

From the outset, the film draws the link between food and death. Moments after he breaks the bad news of the disbandment of his orchestra and admits to concealing the exorbitant price of his cello, Daigo hears Mika screaming from the kitchen. Rushing to check what was going on, he is startled by the sight of a live octopus—a gift from a neighbor—on the floor, its tentacles undulating out of a plastic bag. "It's alive," Mika exclaims. They decide to spare the creature from ending up as their next dinner and release it into the waters of Tokyo Bay, but it is too late. The octopus' lifeless body simply floats away. On one level, there is a symbolic connection between the dead octopus and death of Daigo's career as a cellist. But on another level, the scene serves as an ironic prelude. In the developing story, it will be made clear that the characters have a general revulsion for the remains of the dead,

9. The paroxysmal response to death that marks Filipino funeral rites finds unambiguous, albeit comedic, cinematic representation in two Philippine entries to the Oscar Best Foreign Language Film nominations: *Crying Ladies* (Mark Meily, 2003), and *Grandpa is Dead* (Soxy Topacio, 2009).

viewed for centuries in Japanese culture as ritually impure.[10] Yet, the only acceptable form of animal protein fit for eating (for life) is a dead one. At this stage, the reality of death that is part and parcel of eating animal protein is compartmentalized and sanitized so that the fact that a creature that was once alive was killed for its meat remains hidden from view and systematically forgotten. The association between animal meat and the dead human corpus is obscured. A few scenes forward, after Daigo comes home from the ordeal of encountering a decomposing corpse, yet another gift of food from a neighbor awaits him. Mika cheerfully shows him raw chicken parts on a plate. "Killed fresh this morning," she says, "you could eat it raw." Upon close-up, the fresh-looking parts are neatly piled and arranged, with the severed head as the centerpiece. The sight sends the nauseous Daigo to the sink, gagging and vomiting. Relief comes for him only in intimately caressing Mika's warm body, a frantic effort to re-connect with the living. A repulsive human corpse and an otherwise acceptable animal carcass meant for food find a conscious association: death. Daigo's new experience as an encoffiner is beginning to rend the curtain that separates the pure from the impure but it is nowhere near easy.

Daigo reaches a certain sense of enlightenment during a significant meal scene involving the elder encoffiner Sasaki. Tired and distressed after a tension-filled encoffinment rite, thoughts of quitting crosses Daigo's mind. Yuriko (Kimiko Yo), the administrative assistant, encourages him to have a conversation with the boss. "He's upstairs," she says, pointing up. Noticeable here is the shift in camerawork to a high angle, a worm's eye view, with both Yuriko and Daigo looking vertically up. This suggests that the veteran *nōkanfu* is about to dispense higher wisdom for the apprentice. Going up a flight of stairs and through a sliding door, Daigo enters the residential space of Sasaki. Canopied in lush greenery, it is a cozy oasis of a space compared to the stark office below with its

10. Barbara Hartley cites references indicating the early notion of ritual pollution and the pure/impure dualism that dates back to 8th Century Japan. The two earliest texts are the *Norito*, a compilation of Shinto liturgy, and *Kojiki*, a collection of Japanese mythic history. "Food and Pollution in Two Films from Contemporary Japan," 98.

coffins on display. Sasaki, who is seated at a table set for a meal, invites Daigo to join him.

From Departures © 2010 E1 Entertainment

Two curious egg-shaped pieces of unidentified protein are cooking on a fixed table grill; Sasaki reveals that it is *fugu shirako*, the soft roe of a puffer fish, which is a highly prized delicacy in Japanese cuisine. As he attends to the grill, the older encoffiner shares that the lady in a framed photograph is his late wife. When she died nine years ago, he "made her beautiful," and that inspired him to open his *nōkan* business. Sasaki then proceeds to pick up a *shirako* piece, takes a bite, and relishes the flavor in his mouth. His facial expression, which, up to this point, had been inscrutable, becomes a canvass for pure pleasure. In a word, his reaction is "ecstasy." By all appearances, this to him is the ultimate in *umami*, the Japanese term to describe a savory, sensual taste. Verbally, all Sasaki could say in succumbing to this guilty pleasure is, "It is so good, I hate myself." Interestingly, this echoes a line from the film *Big Night* when virtuoso chef Primo shares his response to his uncle's sumptuous *lasagna bolognese*, "You eat and then. . . you kill yourself, you have to kill yourself, because after you eat this, you can't live!" In between bites, Sasaki waxes philosophical:

SASAKI: Even this (the *shirako*) is a corpse. The living eat the dead. . . unless they're plants. Unless you want to die, you eat. And if you eat, eat well.

Here, Sasaki merely puts into words what had already been signified by the elements that make up the scene's mise-en-scène. Symbolic references of life and death are bedfellows in Sasaki's residential space. His sanctum, bursting with life with its luxuriant indoor plants, has a wintry window view of steady snowfall. It also shares the very same building with his *nōkan* office; a workspace that propounds death with its up front display of coffins and its nondescript interiors. And then there is the food. The sublime flavors of *fugu shirako* is a scrumptious pleasure enjoyed by the living, yet, the delicacy is meat culled from dead marine life. Life and death are not polar realities but two moments of the same cycle. In Japanese Buddhism, the term for this is *shoji*, which *Coffinman* author Shinmon Aoki translates in English as "LifeDeath." Aoki emphasizes that unlike Western thought, which has a tendency to view life and death in dualistic terms, Buddhist thought sees them as a unit. "As far as that goes, the relation of life to death is like the relation of rain to snow in sleet."[11] This motif is further reprised in the form of a montage that appears later in the film.

At this point, we return to the *fugu shirako* eating sequence. After his pithy words, Sasaki invites Daigo to "dig in." When the younger *nōkanfu* obliges and takes a big bite, his expression mirrors that of his mentor. He so delights in the sensual pleasure of eating such an exquisite dish that he too is sent to a state of momentary ecstasy. Sasaki and Daigo's gratifying sensory experience of the ambrosial recalls analogous scenes in the food film classic *Babette's Feast*, and again, in *Big Night*. In the iconic dining scene of *Babette's Feast*, a group of puritans who have sworn to an ascetic distance from all sorts of sensual pleasures, find themselves completely entranced by the extravagant French gourmet dinner prepared by the master chef Babette. Course after sublime course ushers in a freeing experience of gastronomic delight that is akin

---

11. Aoki, *Coffinman*, 30.

to a love affair, ultimately, blurring the divide between spiritual ecstasy and sensual ecstasy so that the words of Psalm 85:10, "righteousness and bliss shall kiss one another" are incarnated at the table. In *Big Night*, the florist Ann samples chef Primo's pasta dish and is similarly overwhelmed with pleasure. "Oh my God. . . oh my God" are the only words she utters, prompting Primo to conclude, "Oh my God is right. Now you know, to eat good food is to get lost to God. . . to have the knowledge of God is the bread of angels." Although the religious dimension hangs farther in the background in the *fugu shirako* scene of *Departures* as compared to the eating scenes in *Babette's Feast* and *Big Night*, they do share a common theme, that of appreciating food as the gift that it truly is, and enjoying the life-affirming pleasures it has to offer, not despite of, but, alongside, the reality of finitude that is our shared heritage as human beings.

Finally, we draw attention to a food scene that serves as an integrative coda to *Departures*. It is important to consider the scene within the context of the larger assemblage of scenes within which it is stylistically and thematically imbricated. The camera establishes that the scene is set in the *nōkan* office on a cold winter night. In a series of close-ups, we see co-workers Sasaki, Daigo, and Yuriko, wolfing down delectable pieces of fried chicken. Each bite is intensely ravenous, as though this was their first good meal in a long time.

From Departures © 2010 E1 Entertainment

The scene is an ironic twist: Daigo devours fried chicken here when earlier, he was nauseated at the very sight of the uncooked parts of the same animal protein. As they grab piece after piece from a serving basket, and dunk bone after bone into a bowl, the camera pulls out to reveal that they are gathered at a small make-shift dining table, a conspicuous plastic Christmas tree with blink-ing lights standing beside it. When Daigo asks Sasaki if he thought the chicken was good, he reprises the words he uttered earlier, "I hate myself." The fried chicken is obviously delicious. The eat-ing frenzy slowing down, Daigo is prodded to play the cello. He fetches a small, scaled down instrument, explaining that it was the cello he used as a child when his dad made him take lessons. When Sasaki had words of affirmation for his dad, Daigo matter of factly dismisses it, saying that his father was "a louse" and "a real bas-tard" for taking off with a waitress who worked in the family café, adding that he is probably dead. In the dialogue that follows, the religious thread clearly interweaves into the narrative fabric. In the sequence, Daigo asks what piece they want him to play and Sasaki's response becomes a verbal cue to the sequence about to unfold:

> SASAKI: Well, since it's Christmas. . .
> DAIGO: Any problems with religious affiliation?
> SASAKI: It's fine. Buddhist, Christian, Islam, Hindu, we handle anything.
> DAIGO: All right, something for a holy night.

Daigo chooses to play "Ave Maria," an 1853 piece by French Ro-mantic composer Charles Gounod based on Johann Sebastian Bach's Prelude No. 1 in C Major. An established favorite for masses, weddings and funerals, the lyrics of the sung version contains the scripture-based "Hail Mary" prayer in Latin. At this juncture, it is not difficult to appreciate the interpretive equation. The Christmas Eve setting and a musical piece dedicated to the Virgin Mary recall the humanity of the mother of Jesus, who was not exempted from the life-death rhythm. Christmas is the definitive celebration of new life, it is the birth of Mary's son, Jesus the Christ, who is the embodiment of an authentic, fully reconciled humanity.[12] But in the fuller paschal story, the image of the mother cradling her infant son is bookended by the image of the *pietà*, the sorrowful mother who cradles the lifeless body of the selfsame son who died on a Roman cross. The life-death rhythm touches all, including a grace-filled woman who is believed to be the mother of God incarnate.

As Daigo plays the moving piece, Sasaki and Yuriko are ushered into a contemplative space, and seamlessly, the music shifts to "Okuribito," the film's soundtrack. The camera pulls out and we are taken outdoors to the snowy panorama of Yamagata where Daigo is shown driving to various encoffinment assignments. The montage confirms Sasaki's statement that in encoffinment, religious affiliation is immaterial. Death being the great equalizer, we see visual representations of Buddhist, Shinto, and Christian elements, but in view of the overt Christmas-Virgin Mary references the film itself proffers, the Christian encoffinment scene holds special significance here. As the western-looking priest pronounces, "We pray in the name of Jesus Christ. Amen," the camera reveals that the deceased is a young boy. There is a distinct pain in suffering the loss of someone who had died at such a young age, and this is dramatized further by the contrasting image of the previous scene where the deceased is an elderly grandmother. The bereaved family's sorrow meaningfully connects with that of the grieving mother Mary, who lost her son in an untimely manner and under cruel circumstances. Mourning the tragic death of a child, they inadvertently image the *mater dolorosa*.

The montage keeps the life-death cycle moving, however, counterbalancing the images of death and mourning with life-affirming allusions. Humor is one notable way by which the sequence achieves this. In one encoffinment scene, the granddaughter of the deceased elderly woman insists that Daigo make her grandmother wear her school socks instead of the traditional leggings, recalling that it was something the latter had always wanted to try on. The girl reveals her grandmother's plucky personality and,

12. Eloquently, Edward Schillebeeckx describes Jesus Christ as the "parable of God and paradigm of humanity." *Jesus*, 626.

in effect, allows a glimmer of her life to shine on her death. In another scene, women of varying generations kiss their departed patriarch goodbye, leaving lipstick marks on his face. A laughing fit breaks through their tears as they express their final thank you to him. Tellingly, the other way by which the montage affirms life is through the image of food. We see scenes that feature Daigo eating in-between calls. He is seated alone at the dining table, carefully squeezing mayonnaise onto one end of an unsliced stick of French bread. He then drizzles soy sauce on a sashimi slice and carefully lays it down on the bread. Before he takes a bite, he plucks a leaf from a potted herb and adds it as a finishing garnish. Noticeable here is Daigo's elegant fingerwork that recalls his artistry in encoffinment; life and death deserve an equally graceful treatment. The life-death motif continues in the scene that immediately follows. While driving to yet another encoffining assignment, Daigo takes a quick bite of *o-nigiri,* a triangular rice cake wrapped in *nori,* or dried seaweed.

It is worth noting that in the montage, the image of Daigo— shot here in wide-angle—playing his cello outdoors against the painterly backdrop of snow-capped Mount Chōkai, is a stylistic strategy that serves to orchestrate the life and death scenes into a beautiful harmonious cycle. However, the cycle is stonewalled when it hits closest to home. Harmony is diminished for as long as Daigo's anger and resentment toward his father threatens to be buried and left unresolved. From the perspective of Japanese Buddhism, this would have considerable implications for *innen,* a notion similar to karma, which is rooted in the belief of the in-terconnectedness of all beings. A dead person who is not given a proper memorial service due to ritual neglect will have an un-happy, suffering spirit; this will cause disturbances and unrest in the lives of the surviving kin.[13] *Departures* closes with the poignant scene when Daigo finds himself face to face with the remains of his long estranged father and performs his encoffinment rite. A flashback scene takes us back to his childhood, at the time when he exchanges letter-stones with his father. The latter's close-ups are

13. Reader, *Religion in Contemporary Japan,* 47–48.

conspicuously off-focus, connoting that Daigo no longer holds his father's face as declarative memory. But Daigo's unexpected discovery of his letter-stone cached in his father's closed hand mellows him and brings him to tears. The scales from his eyes fall so that he is able to recall and recognize the face of the dead man, quickening him to utter the word "father." The dualism between life and death, pure and impure, is overcome.

EAT WELL, LIVE WELL, DIE WELL

The two films spotlighted in this chapter, each following its own narrative direction, hold up to view the connection between food and death. Having established this through an attentive navigation of the contours of the cinematic story, we now explore the thematic impulses that may be brought into range of a Christian theological perspective.

A Simple Life represents food as the way by which the devoted servant Ah Tao expresses maternal care and affection for the man she has helped raise from infancy. The film elevates this to the level of the transcendent by depicting food preparation as a sacrificial expression of a "calling" of sorts, not unlike the fulfillment of religious vows, thus, extending throughout her life, down to her last breath, up until the edge of the mystery of the afterlife where it takes on an eternal character. The gift that keeps on giving, the *amah* will stop at nothing to see Roger live well. Ah Tao's culinary love offering resonates with the notion of "kenosis," or the divine, redemptive self-emptying, which, in Christian theology, is a profoundly trinitarian concept. Theologians such as Karl Rahner and Catherine Mowry LaCugna have proposed that there is no discrepancy between Trinity *in se*, God's inner life in Godself; and Trinity *pro nobis*, God for us.[14] In the divine trinitarian dance that is imaginatively captured by John Damascene's descriptive term "perichoresis," who God is—traditionally, Father, Son, and Holy Spirit—overflows into what God does for us in concrete terms for

14. See Rahner, *The Trinity*, 20–24; and LaCugna, *God For Us*, 1–8.

the sake of our human flourishing. Caught up in the trinitarian perichoresis, we are drawn closer to a fuller, authentic humanity, and ultimately, closer to God. The Trinity then is not just kinetic but kenotic, "a plenitude of self-giving love."[15] This is not to say that Ah Tao's food preparation in *A Simple Life* is trinitarian in any literal sense. The connection is allusive. It is trinitarian in the sense that Ah Tao's cooking, a single-hearted devotion rooted in authentic relationality, is a true gift of self. Yet, the perichoretic movement remains suspended until Roger responds to Ah Tao's gift and, himself, becomes a giver. In his book *Food and Faith: A Theology of Eating*, Norman Wirzba describes true mutuality as a participation in the divine communion:

> To live well, which means to learn to receive gratefully the gifts of others, requires that we also learn to die well by turning our living into a gift for others. Why? Because it is the most fitting acknowledgement of the gifts of life sacrificially given, and our most faithful way of participating in God's own self-offering life as revealed in Christ.

In *A Simple Life*, a trinitarian mutuality finds fuller expression when Roger learns to be a gracious recipient and is moved to be a gift to Ah Tao in his own way. To recall, his care for Ah Tao would primarily take the form of food, the restaurant fare he shares with her during their regular meal outings.

The bone of contention in the Japanese film *Departures* is the traditional understanding of life and death in the dualistic categories of pure and impure. This is dramatized in the social ostracism experienced by the protagonist Daigo who has agreed to work as an encoffiner, an occupation shunned because it involves close contact with the "ritually impure" dead. Daigo's outward journey toward becoming an encoffiner is accompanied by an inner journey, that of coming to an acceptance of life and death as a unitary reality, as "LifeDeath." In more ways than one, food fuels this journey not only in the sense of providing nutritive strength to Daigo,

15. Johnson, *Quest for the Living God*, 214.

but in its capacity to symbolize the paradox that is LifeDeath. "The living eat the dead," the elderly encoffiner Sasaki exclaims between bites of puffer fish roe, clarifying for Daigo that without the death of other organisms, there is no food to eat, and, ultimately, no life. The paradoxical LifeDeath character of food shares resonances with the Christian eucharist. Jesus Christ who "came that they may have life, and have it abundantly" (John 10:10), is the selfsame Jesus Christ who, on a Roman cross, "bowed his head and gave up his spirit (John 19:30). Metaphorized as bread that is broken and wine that is poured out to be shared, Jesus' flesh and blood are offered as spiritual food for the believing community. As theologian Robert Schreiter proposes in his book *In Water and In Blood*, partaking of the bread and wine in the eucharistic meal "becomes a participation in the saving mystery of his death, the saving pathway whereby he opened up the possibility of tasting divine life."[16] The eucharistic communion is LifeDeath par excellence and, even more, a foretaste of a glorious and sumptuous afterlife.

16. Schreiter, *In Water and in Blood*, 95.

5

The Buffet of the Universe

Beasts of the Southern Wild

NO SEASONAL CULINARY RITE is more closely associated with the Louisiana bayou than Cajun seafood boil. Popular in summer backyard cookouts, school events, and church fundraisers, it consists of several pounds of crab, shrimp, or crawfish, or a mess of all three, submerged in a large stock pot of boiling water, and seasoned intuitively with cayenne pepper, salt, bay leaves, and lemon. Potatoes, ears of corn, mushrooms, onions, and garlic, are usually added, rounding out the one-dish meal. Serving and eating the boiled seafood is a tradition all its own. Picnic tables are lined with layers of newspaper and the mess is simply dumped on it and piled high. No utensils needed, partakers simply grab the tasty critters, shell them with their hands, and eat to their hearts content. With plenty of frosty local beer on hand to wash it all down, of course.

Boiled seafood and other fare associated with Louisiana bayou cuisine play a significant role in the creation of meaning in *Beasts of the Southern Wild*, the first feature film of independent filmmaker Behn Zeitlin. Set in a fictional island by the Louisiana levee, the story centers on a hermetically isolated community struggling to preserve their humanity in the aftermath of a cataclysmic hurricane that has a real-life referent in Hurricane Katrina. With a limited budget of $1.2 million and an unlimited imagination, the Queens-born filmmaker moved to New Orleans with a small crew of visionary artists, a collective known as "Court 13," and created an original American folktale that went on to entrance audiences across the globe. An astonishing admixture of small-scale filmmaking and epic-scale myth-making, gritty realism and magic realism, *Beasts of the Southern Wild* was the cinematic miracle at the 2012 Sundance Film Festival where it won the Cinematographic Prize and the Jury Award. Its winning streak would continue at several prestigious international film festivals, the most notable of which was the 2012 Cannes Film Festival where it harvested four awards, including the coveted *Camera D'or*.

Offering rich servings of image and insight, *Beasts of the Southern Wild* is our fitting one-dish-meal in this final chapter of *The Sacred Foodways of Film*.

LIFE IN THE BATHTUB

The Isle de Charles Doucet, "the Bathtub" as locals refer to it, is a floodplain settlement afloat on the southern "wrong side" of the levee that traverses the Louisiana bayou. It is home to a plucky six-year-old girl named Hushpuppy (Quvenzhané Wallis), her high-strung dad Wink (Dwight Henry), and the rest of their close-knit ragtag community. Cut off from mainstream society, life in the Bathtub is characterized by a bohemian, subsistence-level existence sustained by a close dependence on the abundance of the natural world, and a scavenging lifestyle based on the re-purposing of the throwaways of the levee's consumerist other side. Wink has been training his daughter to be a tough survivor, often drawing the growl out of her tiny frame. An intuitive child intimately attuned to nature, Hushpuppy has a special affinity with animals and has a curious habit of listening to their heartbeats. When the schoolteacher and herbalist Miss Bathsheeba (Gina Montana) lectures about the aurochs, an extinct animal believed to have been predatory toward the ancient, cave-dwelling people, Hushpuppy comes up with her own imaginative version of the story. She goes on to narrate how the aurochs once ruled the world and if it had not been for the "iced" age that expunged them, she would have ended up as food for the beasts. "There wouldn't even be a Hush-puppy," she emphasizes, "I would just be breakfast." The rumblings of a gathering storm, a hurricane of apocalyptic proportions, send the Bathtub community into a collective panic. Some flee, a few stay; Wink and Hushpuppy belong to the latter group. As torren-tial rains make a landfall and howling winds batter the scrapwood-and-tinroof backwater landscape, Wink continues to play drill sergeant to a frightened Hushpuppy, barking orders for her to be strong in the eye of the storm. In the aftermath of the hurricane, the Bathtub now reduced to a swampy waterworld, Wink contin-ues to train Hushpuppy in the art of survival. He teaches her how to fish with her bare hands, and when they join other survivors for a meal of boiled shellfish, he orders her to break an entire crab with her bare hands chanting "beast it, beast it, beast it."

From Beasts of the Southern Wild © 2012 Fox Searchlight Pictures

Before long, the community would realize the full extent of the damage wrought by the cataclysm when the high salinity brought in by the storm surge poisons fish and animals. Stuffing the skin of

93

an alligator gar with explosives, Wink and one of the menfolk blow up a section of the levee in order to release the toxic waters. While the drastic measure works and the residents begin to rebuild, it also attracts the authorities who, implementing orders for mandatory evacuation, forcibly relocate the residents into an emergency medical facility. Wink, who had been suffering from an unnamed ailment, undergoes surgery, but his condition only deteriorates. With his daughter and the other evacuees in tow, he escapes the facility and heads back home. Meantime, Hushpuppy and a coterie of young girls her age set out to look for her long lost mother. They swim towards a floating bar named the "Elysian Fields," and, with the help of a boat, succeed in getting there. Aboard the Elysian Fields, Hushpuppy meets a cook, a mysterious woman who, in the child's soft-focus perspective, is her mother. The woman cooks her a meal of fried gator nuggets served with grits, dances with her, and invites her to stay, but Hushpuppy needs to head back to check on her ailing father. Upon her return, a marauding mob of aurochs, awakened by the storm from their frozen state, charge toward her. Without fear, she turns around to face the beasts and looks one of them straight in the eye. Wondrously, she stops them in their tracks and causes them to kneel before her. Given leave to approach her ailing father, Hushpuppy shares with the dying Wink a bite of the fried gator the mysterious mother-figure had cooked. It is their last meal together.

With only minor critical backlash, *Beasts of the Southern Wild* enjoyed near universal praise. The *New York Times*' Manohla Dargis, who screened the film at the 2012 Sundance Film Festival, raved that it was "the standout of this year's Sundance and among the best films to play at the festival in two decades."[1] The enthusiastic response reverberated in many other critical reviews, including that of Dargis's colleague A. O. Scott who declares, "This movie is a blast of sheer, improbable joy, a boisterous, chilling action movie. . ."[2] Similarly entranced, Los Angeles Times critic Betsy Sharkey writes, "This is a remarkably skilled first feature for the filmmakers

1. Dargis, "Amazing Child, Typical Grown-ups," para. 4.
2. Scott, "She's the Man of the Swamp," para. 10.

and its fusion of fable and soulful reality has been widely embraced on the festival circuit. . ."[3]

What is the creative alchemy that makes *Beasts of the Southern Wild* a film of such astonishing beauty and power? For the purposes of this chapter, four key aspects merit our attention.

First of these is the film's visionary screenplay, a folkloric narrative that germinated from filmmaker Benh Zeitlin's initial inspiration to tell the story of Louisiana residents who chose not to evacuate their homes despite prescient warnings of Hurricane Katrina's likely impact. Partnering with playwright Lucy Alibar, Zeitlin picked up some basic elements of the latter's one-act play *Juicy and Delicious* and his own previous short film *Glory at Sea*, and allowed the material to develop organically into an audacious, soulful piece of bayou folklore. Zeitlin, in fact, grew up in an environment that encouraged an early appreciation for grassroots culture; both his parents are professional folklorists at the New York-based organization City Lore. Through the narrative weave of folklore, *Beasts of the Southern Wild* makes visible the cosmic-spiritual dimension of eco-human existence.

The second aspect is the film's sets and settings, which evoke a strong visceral sense of a struggling, post-apocalyptic bayou culture. Zeitlin builds the landscape of the fictional Bathtub community out of the detritus of a post-Katrina Louisiana, literally piecing together found objects and scrap material to create a world cohabited by squalor—the devastation and impoverishment in the aftermath of the hurricane—and bounty—the abundance of natural resources in the floodplain. In the bricolage that is the Bathtub, an abandoned trailer propped by discarded oil drums is a home, the body of a pick-up truck motored by old lawn mower engines is a means of transportation, and nature's gift of fish and shellfish swarming by the net-full or swimming directly into one's hands is a meal. The Bathtub floodplain represents a liminal space, a paradoxical threshold of lived chaos and envisioned cosmos. It is, at one and the same time, a place and an idea.

3. Sharkey, "Review: Emotional 'Beasts of the Southern Wild' is Extraordinary," para. 3.

The third aspect is the authenticity of the characters that inhabit the Bathtub. Resolute, eccentric, and unadorned by the self-conscious trappings of "civilization," the truthful, flesh-and-blood characters owe much to Zeitlin's purposeful strategy of casting natural talents who had no previous acting experience. The non-professional actors such as Dwight Henry—a baker in real life—who plays the character of Hushpuppy's father Wink, were plucked from the talent pool offered by the local bayou communities. The casting miracle, of course, is Quvenzhané Wallis who was only five years old at the time of the auditions; she was singled out from a field of four thousand girls to play the lead role. Gifted with mettle, charisma, and raw talent, Wallis, in more ways than one, embodies Hushpuppy. She went on to become the youngest Best Actress nominee in Oscar history, a record she still holds. Zeitlin describes Wallis as "looking like a warrior," and adds that the little girl "wasn't exactly how we had imagined the character, but her spirit was the spirit of the movie." In fact, the strategy of casting real people such as Wallis who actually live in the Gulf Coast establishes a dynamic equivalence between them and the characters they play. More than simply performing roles, they reveal the true, defiant spirit of bayou life, and invite the audience in. Across the board, critics and audiences had a favorable review of the cast in general, but a native informant's validation carries special weight. An entry from a southern Louisiana native in the *Cajun Tomato* blog reads:

> As I watched *Beasts of the Southern Wild.* . . I swelled with pride at the sight of my south Louisiana homeland and its residents portrayed on the silver screen in an accurate manner—perhaps outgunned by nature and other manmade forces but resilient and awash with *joie de vivre* to the bitter end.

Finally, the fourth aspect of the film, one that holds particular relevance to our project, is its representation of foodways. From a steaming basketful of Cajun seafood boil upended on a table, to fried gator nuggets served with grits, food enjoys a fair degree of omnipresence in *Beasts of the Southern Wild*. In the narrative, food does not simply offer bodily nutrition, it also serves as the tangible and edible expression of the condition of the characters' most integral relationships through the ebb and flow of events and experiences that mark their lives. With an awareness of the ways by which all four elements work together in a creative conspiracy, we bring to sharper focus the aspect of foodways.

FOOD FIGHTS, FOOD CONNECTIONS

We are all Meat

The classroom scene opens with the schoolteacher Bathsheeba lecturing in Cajun slang as she looks intently at Hushpuppy and other pupils through the basket in front of her containing an overspill of live, wriggling crawfish.

> BATHSHEEBA: Meat. Meat. Meat. Every animal is made out of meat. I'm meat, y'all asses meat. Everything is part of the buffet of the universe.

Today's lesson is clear: just as crawfish is meat to human beings and other creatures higher up the food chain, so are human beings to the infinitely larger forces of the universe. When a rogue crawfish escapes the basket and crawls away, Bathsheeba snatches it and tosses it back, visualizing another lesson: there is no escape from the cosmic reality that "everything is part of the buffet of the universe." The teacher then shows her pupils an image tattooed on her leg. Resembling a cave painting, it depicts spear-wielding early humans struggling to fend off colossal horned animals known as the aurochs, yet one more visual validation of her previous point.

> BATHSHEEBA: This here is an aurochs. A fierce, mean creature that roamed the earth back when we all lived in caves. They would gobble the cave-babies down right in front of their cave-parents. And the cave-mens couldn't even do nothing about it because they was too poor, too stupid, too small.

That this represents fuzzy science—aurochs were the herbivorous precursors of modern cattle, and were endemic to Europe through the seventeenth century—is beside the point; in this creative appropriation, humans were meat to the aurochs. Bathsheeba then widens the aperture and draws a present-day parallel. Pointing to a map of the levee with the Bathtub on the south side, she asserts:

> BATHSHEEBA: Any day now, fabric of the universe is coming unraveled. Ice cap's gonna melt, water's gonna rise, and everything south of the levee is going under. Y'all better learn how to survive now.

The savage aurochs is equated with the calamitous backlash of climate change. In the face of such a monstrous catastrophe that threatens to devour everything in its path, human beings are precisely what Bathsheeba had described them—meat. Yet, the film suggests that human beings are complicit in the acceleration of climate change and, ultimately, implicated in the melting of the polar ice caps. This is depicted in the contrasting images of the two sides of the levee. On the "wrong side" with its marsh and mud landscape, and scavenging lifestyle, the Bathtub has a more immediate and sustainable connection with the natural world. Hushpuppy's unusual habit of listening to heartbeats, not just of people, but also of animals, poetically represents this vital connection. In contrast, the developed "dry side" has an industrialized landscape of concrete and steel, connoting its dependence on the cycle of production-consumption, a known culprit of greenhouse gas emissions. "Ain't that ugly over there," Wink would comment to Hushpuppy as their makeshift boat passes by and catches a view of the developed other side with its manufacturing plants that cough out thick smoke. We then hear Hushpuppy's voiceover as she narrates:

> HUSHPUPPY: Daddy says, up above the levee, on the dry side, they're afraid of the water like a bunch of babies. They built the wall that cuts us off.

The concrete levee symbolizes the separation between the Bathtub community and the dry side, and, beyond that, its distance and alienation from the natural world. It prevents it from hearing nature's heartbeat.

Reconciling Foodways

Meaningfully, the Bathtub community's intimate relationship with nature is expressed in food. In the film's introductory sequence, Wink is forking a whole fresh chicken–head and feet included– from an icebox, onto a grill. Then we see father and daughter partaking of the meal in a barn along with farm animals and dogs. There is no table set-up, let alone plates and silverware. Hushpuppy is seated on the dirt floor eating a huge chunk of the chicken carcass and throwing some to the animals. Wink throws corn kernels to the chickens while instructing the girl to share some of the chicken meat with the dogs. The manner of food consumption here discloses an unspoken acceptance of the natural food web: living beings derive food from other living beings, and in turn, serve as food for other living beings. The imagery brings to mind kindred scenes in the Mexican film *Alamar* (Pedro González-Rubio, 2009), which is set in a tiny fishing community in Banco Chinchorro, the second-largest coral reef on earth, and one of the rare few with an ecosystem still uninjured. The meal scenes in *Alamar* take place in a rustic wood cabin propped on stilts in the water. Here, seabirds and marine crocodiles are co-partakers of the freshly caught and cooked barracuda and lobster from a dinner table set for a four-year-old boy, his father, and his grandfather, both of whom are subsistence fishermen. These mutually analogous scenes in *Beasts of the Southern Wild* and *Alamar* reflect an essential intimacy with nature; austere and countercultural, the meal is organic in its very food, its setting, and its inclusion of animals in the activity of eating.

A more consistent cinematic representation of the Bathtub's near-primeval dependence on the fruit of the earth can be seen in the visual motif of a "big catch," a number of scenes where the camerawork focuses on the bounty of the bayou. We see this early in the film during the celebratory montage sequence where images of the Bathtub's holiday merrymaking are intercut with various snippets of its daily activities. A fishing net releases its catch on a wooden trough, and in close-up, the camera pans to reveal a generous haul of live fish, crab, shrimp, and crawfish. Hushpuppy looks at the wriggling critters with great curiosity while Wink is preoccupied with sorting them. The big catch in this sequence represents a reasonable dependence on the bounty of the bayou; the community catches what it needs for the survival of its members. It is not by any stretch comparable to commercial fishing and its processed products that fill supermarket shelves. Hushpuppy issues an oblique indictment of the latter when she narrates:

> HUSHPUPPY: Daddy's always saying that back in the dry world, they've got none of what we've got. . . they've got fish stuck in plastic wrappers. . .

Relevantly, a later scene provides dramatic contrast to the alienation from nature symbolized by "fish stuck in plastic wrappers." From his makeshift boat, Wink demonstrates to his daughter a strangely off-kilter way of fishing that simply involves sticking a hand into the water and waiting for fish to swim right into it. In a matter of seconds, a fat catfish materializes in his hand.

From Beasts of the Southern Wild © 2012 Fox Searchlight Pictures

The clever, restrained magic realism in the scene suggests that the proximity between the Bathtub and the natural world is not merely a spatial and physical connection, it is a mystical bond. One way by which the film validates this mystical bond is through negation. When the characters have to deal with food that is commercially processed and not organically derived, they are placed in a context of negativity or suspicion. One such scene unfolds early in the film when Hushpuppy could not find Wink and has to prepare a meal for herself. The pot of bubbling goulash she is cooking on the stovetop, a disgusting mixture of canned soup and canned cat food, explodes violently when she turns up the heat. In another instance, in the emergency medical facility after the forced evacuation, a close-up shot of the rationed meal shows a piece of processed food that is so nondescript, it defies identification. Wink sternly orders Hushpuppy not to eat it. In what could be construed as an asceticism that is not unlike the practice of religious abstinence, Wink's reaction suggests that the Bathtub community considers processed food, food that is not sourced directly from the providence of the earth, as unfit for consumption. Because it had been offered at the altar of the commercial assembly line on the other side of the levee, it is defiled. Eating such food would constitute a breach of the intimate human-nature relationship.

On a more interpersonal level, food and drink in *Beasts of the Southern Wild* serve as a unifying force that draws the Bathtub dwellers together as they face human and natural challenges that threaten to break them apart as a community. We are first introduced to the Bathtub in an early sequence when the residents are celebrating an undisclosed holiday, one of many, as Hushpuppy would narrate. In random *mardi gras* fashion, they are engaged in exuberant revelry–running and shouting, riding vehicles decorated with scavenged material, playing musical instruments, and drinking booze like there's no tomorrow. The celebration is a form of defiant, communitarian self-assertion, an affirmation of life before the coming of the perfect storm.

As mentioned earlier, a community feast of seafood boil would mark the storm's immediate aftermath. The partakers are the remnant who had the strength to "beast it;" those who remained in the Bathtub, braved the rising waters, and lived another day to enjoy the rich and delicious food that the bayou offers. The same remnant would re-group as a floating boat community. They decide to live together in a houseboat, taking with them various live animals, potted greens, and other provisions, in a self-sustaining Noah's Ark arrangement.

A more clarified imaging of the reconciling power of food emerges when we follow the relational triad between Hushpuppy, her father Wink, and her mother who remains an elusive, mysterious presence. When we are first allowed to take a glimpse of the image of Hushpuppy's mother, it is by way of Wink's mythic storytelling—notably imbued with culinary metaphors—retold from the child's memory. In a hazy flashback sequence, we learn that Wink falls in love with the woman who literally saves his life, shooting an alligator on the prowl while he was taking a nap outdoors. We see that she is a curvy woman, but the camera only shows her from the neck down so that we never get a glimpse of her face. What we do know from Wink's recollection is that she is so beautiful that she can magically ignite stove burners and cause pots of water to boil, just by her presence. Wink would then note that the felled alligator ends up as their meal, all battered up and fried by the woman. There is no indication in the narrative as to why Hushpuppy's mother is no longer with them in the Bathtub, but it is clear that she is fondly and vividly remembered, most especially by her daughter.

Re-visiting in greater detail the latter part of *Beasts of the Southern Wild* when Hushpuppy and a bunch of girls are taken aboard the floating bar Elysian Fields, we gain fuller insight on the role of food as a pathway to reconciliation for Hushpuppy and her parents. As Hushpuppy makes her way through the bar, it looks like she had stepped into a bizarre dreamworld. Gaudy foil curtains and blinking party lights everywhere. Flamboyant bar girls young and old, drinking and dancing with their partners. Jazz singers with muffled voices. And a haze of cigarette-smoke hanging heavily in the air. The surreal images flash in the girl's line of vision until she reaches the end of the room and encounters an attractive woman guzzling a bottle of cold beer; judging from her apron, she is presumably a cook. In the previous flashback scenes, Hushpuppy's mother is consistently shown downing beer from the bottle; although inconclusive, the association is hard to ignore. When they are face to face, a second connection is hinted. "Get in here, let me show you a magic trick," the woman tells her. Pushing through a double door entrance, she leads Hushpuppy into a barely visible space enveloped in thick fog. Stylistically, the scene is an invitation for us to enter into Hushpuppy's imaginative point of view; in the child's wishful understanding, she has found her mother, the magical woman who can ignite fires without even trying. Further connections become apparent the moment it is revealed what the "magic trick" is all about. She is going to prepare a meal for Hushpuppy, but as the little girl would witness, this is no ordinary meal. The woman takes an egg, magically blows off the top of its shell, and pours the content into a bowl. Then in close-up, the camera focuses on her hands as she slices a gator tail, separating the meat from the grotesque scaly armor. Taking the pieces of white meat, she dunks them in batter and sets them out on a heated pan to fry. While cooking, the woman dispenses grown-up advice to Hushpuppy. Using food metaphors to drive her point, she warns Hushpuppy that when her food falls down on the floor, no one will pick it up for her, so she had better learn to smile and be strong because no one respects a self-pitying person. What becomes apparent in this meaningful depiction of image and insight is that the woman's message is the maternal explanation of what Wink had been teaching Hushpuppy all along: "beast it!" With those words of wisdom, she puts a few of the cooked gator nuggets on a plate of grits and serves the meal to the girl. That this woman may well be her mother becomes even more convincing. To recall Wink's storytelling, fried gator was the very dish Hushpuppy's mother prepared for her father; in a manner of speaking, it was the dish that saved his life. All this had not been lost to Hushpuppy. Past the rampaging aurochs whom she was able to connect with in a profound manner, she brings some of the fried gator from the Elysian Fields to her bedridden father. With great care and gentleness, she takes a piece and feeds it to Wink. In that one quiet moment, Hushpuppy brings her family together, if not in a literal sense, in a profound, symbolic sense. Her mother's magical gator dish, yet again, saves.

Untamed Nature

As a relevant postscript to our exploration of food and its meaning in the cinematic narrative, it is necessary for us to discuss in some detail the continuing motif of "untamed nature," an important piece to understanding the lead characters' motivations and actions. In spite of the profound, mystical bond between the bathtub residents and nature, the latter cannot be domesticated. When there is a denial and lack of respect for this incontestable reality, nature has a way of "fighting back" to reassert its unfettered, fearsome power. *Beasts of the Southern Wild* represents this symbolically through the imaginative, puerile perspective of Hushpuppy. After the young girl accidentally sets her shack on fire, father and daughter bursts into an angry exchange:

> WINK: I have to worry about you all the damn time, you're killing me! You're killing me! Get up now and come on!
>
> HUSHPUPPY: I hope you die, and when you're dead, I'll go to your grave and eat birthday cake all by myself!

Angry and defiant, Hushpuppy gives Wink a jab, right on the left side of his chest where his heart is. There is a symbolic resonance in this; to recall, Hushpuppy has a habit of listening to heartbeats. She is not listening this time. Wink, who has been struggling with an ailment, staggers and falls; immediately, we hear peals of thunder booming from the darkening sky. As the startled Hushpuppy looks down at her unconscious dad and looks up to the ominous canopy of clouds, flash-cuts of massive Antarctic glaciers collapsing into the sea punctuate the scene. Fleeing until she reaches the shoreline of the bayou, Hushpuppy utters these words in a manner not unlike prayer: "Mama, I think I broke something!" On the level of denotation, she is speaking to her absentee mother, an organic turn considering that the young girl has been portrayed as harboring a deep longing for maternal care. Her desire for mothering will be reprised at a later turn when she seeks out her mother after Wink's condition worsens and he is on the brink of death. That being said, the scene invites a second, connotational interpretation. In view of the juxtaposed images of collapsing glaciers, not to mention the child's special affinity with nature's heartbeat, it is within reason to propose that Hushpuppy is also addressing her other mama: Mother Nature. In this profoundly moving scene, Hushpuppy inadvertently confesses the collective human "sin" against Mother Nature. "Mama, I think *we* broke something!" is the message sublimated beneath her actual words. Human complicity has disrupted the natural harmony of the earth, and the gathering tempest is an eloquent testament to nature's fury.

To be sure, the most cinematic representation of fearsome, unbridled nature in the film is the aurochs. Coming back from the dead when the glaciers crumble, they are shown charging headlong in search of food and flattening structures that stand in their way. When one of them collapses and dies, the rest turn cannibals and have a meal of it. The aurochs may be interpreted as a symbolic materialization of the ferocious power and sheer enormousness of nature as pictured in the mind of an imaginative child. They represent Hushpuppy's primal fear of being meat, easy prey to the vast and untamed universe. In an interview with National Geographic, Zeitlin emphasizes that the aurochs is Hushpuppy's imaginative way of making sense of the chaos around her:

> I think [the aurochs' meaning] evolves over the course of the film. At the beginning, Hushpuppy's relationship with nature is that she's a morsel of food that's going to be consumed by a larger force. The only way she understands death is a big thing eating a smaller thing—the food chain. All the things that are bigger than her and that have created her are being consumed by things bigger than them—her father being consumed by his illness, her home being consumed by storms and floods and

saltwater intrusion and land loss. That violent relationship is the way she begins her understanding of nature.[4]

Nature is a blessing, but it is also a beast. But so is Hushpuppy. The
girl has been trained to "beast it," to be strong and fearless in the
eye of the storm, be it a literal one that submerges her home community in floodwaters, a figurative one that threatens to take away
her only parent and make a complete orphan out of her, or a
mytho-prehistoric one in the form of rampaging beasts that are
poised to attack and overpower her. She herself is a force of nature,
untamed and formidable. In her "wild" moments, she breaks open
a whole crab with her bare hands, blows up into flames her own
shack, and takes the lead in swimming quite a distance to reach a
floating bar further out the bayou. Most revealingly, she punches
her father in the heart, a dramatic departure from her usual sensitive habit of listening to heartbeats.

From Beasts of the Southern Wild © 2012 Fox Searchlight Pictures

Although her diminutive size belies the beast in her, the aurochs
themselves recognize Hushpuppy's true nature when they encounter her face to face. Not only do they literally see eye to eye, they
acknowledge her as the Alpha-beast and kneel before her. Here,
there is a striking parallel between Hushpuppy and Paikea, the
girl-heroine in the comparable folkloric film *Whale Rider* (Niki

4. Berlin, "The Story Behind 'Beasts of the Southern Wild,'" para. 4.

Caro, New Zealand, 2002). In the latter's story world, whales are mythical creatures that embody the spirits of the Maori ancestors. When the villagers find a great number of them beached one day, they interpret it as a bad omen. Koro, the tribal chief, blames his own granddaughter Paikea (Keisha Castle-Hughes) for the tragic phenomenon of nature that had befallen them. The custodian of his tribe's patriarchal leadership, he has fiercely objected to all intimations that Paikea is the chosen one to become the tribe's future chief.[5] The community's heroic efforts to push the whales back into the ocean prove futile, but to everyone's amazement, it is the young girl who is able to communicate with the marine giants on some mystical plane. Face to face with the lead whale, she is able to ride on its back and command it to swim into the ocean while the rest of the stranded whales follow suit. In both *Whale Rider* and *Beasts of the Southern Wild*, the relationship between the lead characters—both of whom are young girls who defy the muscular, patriarchal ideal of strength, by embodying the power of vulnerability and spirituality—and the natural world, is profoundly mystical. They are conjoined in the wordless depths.

A DEEP COMMUNION

From the tiniest to the largest, all things in the universe co-exist in a living web of interdependence; this is the heart of the matter shared by the film *Beasts of the Southern Wild* and ecotheology. Drawing from science, Rosemary Radford Ruether's *Gaia and God: An Ecofeminist Theology of Earth Healing*, plumbs the depths of this interdependence down to the subatomic level, an "absolute minimum," where the matter-energy distinction no longer holds. This "void-like web" is where the vast universe finds its primary interconnection:

> As we move below the "absolute minimum" of the tini-
> est particles into the dancing void of energy patterns

5. In chapter 8 of my previous book, I offer an in-depth discussion of *Whale Rider* from the interpretive lens of the Christ-figure. See Sison, *World Cinema, Theology, and the Human*, 121–38.

that build up the "appearance" of solid objects on the macroscopic level, we also recognize that this is also the "absolute maximum," the matrix of all interconnections of the whole universe.[6]

Said differently, we are all made out of the same "stuff," and at this most basic level, the tapestry of the universe is knitted together. We have devoted ample attention to the examination of the human-and-nature relationship in *Beasts of the Southern Wild*, portrayed in the Bathtub community's close dependence on the natural world for sustenance, and more poetically, in the mysticism of Hushpuppy's attunement to the heartbeat of living beings. In a more specific way, the oneness of the very big and the very small is imaged in Hushpuppy's unusual connectedness with the aurochs, which is brought to fullness in their eventual face-to-face encounter. "We're friends, kinda," Hushpuppy would affirm, after the gigantic beasts kneel before the tiny child in acknowledgement of their kinship. In the film's penultimate sequence, the funeral rite for Wink where Hushpuppy leads the cremation of his body and its release to the bayou on his old boat, we hear the girl's voiceover narration meaningfully resonating with Ruether's words:

> HUSHPUPPY: When it all goes quiet behind my eyes, I see everything that made me flying around in invisible pieces. When I look too hard, it goes away. But when it all goes quiet, I see they're right here. I see that I am a little piece of a big, big universe. And that makes things right.

From the perspective of ecotheology, the profound level of interconnectedness is the very ground within which the divine presence is made manifest. Pope Francis makes this point in his 2015 encyclical *Laudato Si—Praise be to you: On Care for our Common Home*:

> In this universe, shaped by open and intercommunicating systems, we can discern countless forms of relationship and participation. This leads us to think of the

---

6. Ruether, *Gaia and God*, 248.

whole as open to God's transcendence, within which it develops.[7]

God is the animating principle of all living things; the divine activity in the created universe is "in the order of God's love." But Pope Francis asserts that the authenticity of this order is at stake when it is not incarnated in the human community. "A sense of deep communion with the rest of nature cannot be real if our hearts lack tenderness, compassion, and concern for our fellow humans."[8] Communion with the natural world and communion with fellow human beings are coterminous, they are mutually inclusive realities. As we have previously discussed, the bayou dwellers of *Beasts of the Southern Wild* evince both an affinity with nature and with each other. A thriving communitarian spirit is evident in the earnest kinship between the Bathtub residents; they are an extended family of survivors, in solidarity with each other and with the natural world they call home.

Inspirited by the kinetic presence of the divine, the interrelationships within the eco-human family may be described as a trinitarian perichoresis. As described in the previous chapter, the term was proposed by St. John Damascene to describe the life-giving dance of the one God who is an eternal communion of three, pouring out into the created universe, and back again into the eternal communion. Caught up in the rhythm of the trinitarian perichoresis, the created universe is nothing less than a sacrament, God's love made manifest in historical visibility. But if the created universe moves in the perichoretic order of God's love, why is eco-human existence, as we know it, marked by alienation, brokenness, and violence? The telltale signs of a breakdown of authentic relationality are everywhere in *Beast of the Southern Wild*: radical climate change and the human complicity that multiplies its destructiveness, the wall of alienation between the bayou side and the industrial side of the levee, the law of predation where all living things in nature are ultimately "meat," broken families

7. Pope Francis, *Laudato Si—Praise be to You*, 34.
8. Ibid., 38.

emblematized by Hushpuppy's missing mother. A death-dealing, counter-choreography seems to be at work to sabotage the fragile eco-human communion. Understood from the lens of Christian ecotheology, the natural world in its disjointedness and finitude carries an implicit appeal to a promised wholeness. In *Quest for the Living God: Mapping Frontiers in the Theology of God*, feminist theologian Elizabeth Johnson ponders on the same question and offers relevant insight. From the evolving universe, there emerges a "cruciform pattern," the inescapable reality of creatureliness and death experienced on all levels of created existence. Yet, this cruciform pattern is a paschal pattern, "cross and resurrection rediscovered on a cosmic scale."[9] The stigmata of suffering and death are not the last word; the vision of a definitively reconciled universe rises in the horizon as a promise. The Creator Spirit is not finished with us yet. Meantime, the perichoretic dance continues to imbue the universe with a grace-filled wholeness, fragmentary in the meantime, made complete in the eschatological future.

Within the cruciform pattern that characterizes *Beasts of the Southern Wild*, a taste of the promised wholeness and reconciliation is symbolically expressed in food. In the immediate aftermath of the fearsome hurricane that obliterates their island home, the Bathtub dwellers are drawn to re-group around the dinner table for a plentiful feast of boiled seafood. It is around this paradoxical table that they find renewed strength, here represented by the community's united voice that helps empower Hushpuppy to "beast it;" by extension, it is a call-out to the younger generation to be strong and resilient as they face a future bereft of certitude. The other significant meal of reconciliation, as we have already examined in detail, is the shared meal of fried gator, first prepared by Hushpuppy's mother when she saved Wink's life, then served to Hushpuppy by the mysterious mother-figure in the floating bar, and finally shared by Hushpuppy to Wink on his deathbed. It's noteworthy that all three sequences portraying the gator meal are immersed in a surreal atmosphere, offering a window to a deeper level of meaning. This is particularly significant in the third sequence

9. Johnson, *Quest for the Living God*, 190.

when Hushpuppy offers a piece of gator to the dying Wink, not in the usual boisterous Bathtub manner, but in a solemnized gesture that recalls a communion ritual. There is close framing of father and daughter so that as they face each other, we see the meaningful poetics of their gaze.

From Beasts of the Southern Wild © 2012 Fox Searchlight Pictures

In wordless quietude, Hushpuppy opens the packed food, takes a piece of gator, and gently brings it into Wink's mouth. She then takes a piece herself and partakes of the meal with him. The fried gator meal is symbolically shared in a fragile perichoresis, upholding the symbolic oneness of the trinity of father, mother, daughter.

The fellowship of sharing a meal within a cruciform pattern has profound eschatological resonances. It is an anticipation of a coming banquet, an ever-expanding table fellowship that nourishes, heals, reconciles, and saves. At the head of the table is the Lord of the feast, the infinitely loving and gracious host, who welcomes all to the buffet of the universe.

Bibliography

Allen, John S. *The Omnivorous Mind: Our Evolving Relationship with Food.* Cambridge: Harvard University Press, 2012.

Aoki, Shinmon. *Coffinman: The Journal of a Buddhist Mortician.* Translated by Wayne S. Yokoyama. Anaheim, CA: Buddhist Education Center, 2002.

Auden, W.H. "On Installing an American Kitchen in Lower Austria." *The New Yorker*, March 7, 1959.

Barbotin, Edmond. *The Humanity of Man.* Translated by Matthew J. O'Connell. Maryknoll, NY: Orbis, 1975.

Baron, Cynthia, Diane Carson, and Mark Bernard. *Appetites and Anxieties: Food, Film, and the Politics of Representation.* Detroit: Wayne State University Press, 2013.

Berlin, Jeremy. "The Story Behind *Beasts of the Southern Wild.*" *National Geographic* (July 17, 2012). http://voices.nationalgeographic. com/2012/07/17/the-story-behind-beasts-of-the-southern-wild/.

Boff, Leonardo. *Jesus Christ Liberator: A Critical Christology of Our Time.* Translated by Patrick Hughes. Maryknoll, NY: Orbis, 1997.

Bovon, François. *Luke 2: A Commentary on the Gospel of Luke 9:51–19:27.* Translated by Donald S. Deer. Minneapolis: Fortress, 2013.

Brady, Tara. "A Simple Life/*Tao Jie.*" *The Irish Times* (August 3, 2012). http://www.irishtimes.com/culture/film/a-simple-life-tao-jie-1.529875?mode=print&ot=example.AjaxPageLayout.ot.

Brook, Jane, ed. *Kitchen Wit: Quips and Quotes for Cooks and Food Lovers.* Chichester, UK: Summersdale, 2009.

Collier, Paul. *The Bottom Billion: Why the Poorest Countries are Failing and What Can be Done About It,* 3–14. New York: Oxford University Press, 2008.

Dargis, Manohla. "Amazing Child, Typical Grown-ups." *The New York Times* (January 27, 2012). http://www.nytimes.com/2012/01/28/movies/at-sundance-beasts-of-the-southern-wild-is-standout.html?_r=0.

Francis, Pope. *Laudato Si—Praise be to You: On Care for our Common Home.* Vatican: Libreria Editrice Vaticana, 2015.

Freedman, David Noel, ed. *The Anchor Bible Dictionary.* Vol. 1. New York: Doubleday, 1992.

Gritten, David. "*Departures* is Not What People Expect from Japanese Cinema." *The Telegraph* (November 20, 2009). http://www.telegraph. co.uk/journalists/david-gritten/6598274/Departures-is-not-what-people-expect-from-Japanese-cinema.html.

Hartley, Barbara. "Food and Pollution in Two Films from Contemporary Japan." *IJPS* 8 (2012) 98–106. http://ijaps.usm.my/wp-content/uploads/2012/07/BHartley-Food-Pollution.pdf .

Johnson, Elizabeth. *Quest for the Living God: Mapping Frontiers in the Theology of God.* New York: Continuum, 2007.

Keller, James. *Food, Film, and Culture.* Jefferson, NC: McFarland, 2006.

Klass, Dennis. "Grief and Mourning in Cross-Cultural Perspective." *Encyclopedia of Death and Dying.* http://www.deathreference.com/Gi-Ho/Grief-and-Mourning-in-Cross-Cultural-Perspective.html.

LaCugna, Catherine Mowry. *God For Us: The Trinity and Christian Life,* 1–8. New York: HarperCollins, 1991.

Lee, Edmund. "A Simple Life." *Time Out: Hong Kong* (March 8, 2012). http://www.timeout.com.hk/film/features/49124/a-simple-life.html.

Lowen, Linda. "Feminism in India–Conversation with Indian Feminist Sarojini Sahoo." *About.com.* http://womensissues.about.com/od/feminismequalrights/a/FeminisminIndia.htm.

Malina, Bruce. *The New Testament World: Insights from Cultural Anthropology.* Revised ed. Louisville: Westminster/John Knox, 1993.

Mazzoni, Cristina. *The Women in God's Kitchen: Cooking, Eating, and Spiritual Writing.* New York: Continuum, 2005.

Moskin, Julia. "A Change in the Kitchen." *The New York Times* (January 21, 2014). http://www.nytimes.com/.

Neruda, Pablo. *Love: Ten Poems.* New York: Miramax, 1995.

Ochsner, Gina. "Filled to Brokenness: Notes to Hunger." In *The Spirit of Food: 34 Writers on Feasting and Fasting Toward God,* edited by Leslie Leyland Fields, 149–159. Eugene, OR: Cascade, 2010.

O'Collins, Gerald. *Jesus: A Portrait.* Maryknoll: Orbis, 2008.

Okuyama, Yoshiko. "Shinto and Buddhist Metaphors in *Departures.*" *Journal of Religion and Film* 17 (April 2013) 4–5. http://digitalcommons.unomaha.edu/cgi/viewcontent.cgi?article=1065&context=jrf.

Parker-Bowles, Tom. "Anyone for Filipino?." *Esquire: UK* (August 2011), 87.

Rahner, Karl. *The Trinity,* 20–24. Translated by Joseph Donceel. New York: Crossroad, 1970.

Ratzinger, Joseph. *Jesus of Nazareth: From the Baptism in the Jordan to the Transfiguration.* Translated by Adrian J. Walker. San Francisco: Doubleday, 2007.

Remnick, David. *Secret Ingredients: The New Yorker Book of Food and Drink.* New York: Modern Library, 2008.

Rosenbaum, Ron. "Anthony Bourdain's Theory on the Foodie Revolution," *Smithsonian* (December 3, 2014). http://www.smithsonianmag.com/arts-culture/anthony-bourdains-theory-foodie-revolution-180951848/?no-ist

Ruether, Rosemary Radford. *Gaia and God: An Ecofeminist Theology of Earth Healing*. Anniversary ed. New York: HarperCollins, 1993.

———. *Sexism and God-Talk: Toward a Feminist Theology*. Boston: Beacon Press, 1983.

Reader, Ian. *Religion in Contemporary Japan*. Honolulu: University of Hawaii Press, 1991.

Russell, Sharman Apt. *Hunger: An Unnatural History*. New York: Basic, 2005.

Sanjukta, Sharma. "Film Review: *The Lunchbox*." *Live Mint* (September 19, 2013). http://www.livemint.com/Leisure/lj3jHG8yUngGOBWcabpDDP/Film-review—The-Lunchbox.html.

Schillebeeckx, Edward. *Jesus: An Experiment in Christology*. Translated by Hubert Hoskins. New York: Crossroad, 1979.

Schmemman, Alexander. *For the Life of the World: Sacraments and Orthodoxy*. New York: Athens, 1982.

Schreiter, Robert J. *In Water and in Blood: A Spirituality of Solidarity and Hope*. Revised ed. Maryknoll, NY: Orbis, 2006.

Scott, A.O. "She's the Man of the Swamp." *The New York Times* (June 26, 2012). http://www.nytimes.com/2012/06/27/movies/beasts-of-the-southern-wild-directed-by-benh-zeitlin.html.

Shapiro, Eben. "A Harvard Study Spices Bollywood Romance in 'The Lunchbox.'" *IndiaRealTime* (April 2, 2014). http://blogs.wsj.com/indiarealtime/2014/04/03/a-harvard-study-spices-bollywood-romance-the-lunchbox/.

Sharkey, Betsy. "Review: Emotional 'Beasts of the Southern Wild' is Extraordinary." *Los Angeles Times* (July 26, 2012). http://touch.latimes.com/#section/-1/article/p2p-73821718/.

Sison, Antonio D. *World Cinema, Theology, and the Human: Humanity in Deep Focus*. New York: Routledge, 2012.

St. Michel, Patrick. "Crying it Out in Japan." *The Atlantic* (May 2015). http://www.theatlantic.com/magazine/archive/2015/05/crying-it-out-in-japan/389528/.

Thomke, Stefan. "Mumbai's Model of Service Excellence." *Harvard Business Review* (November 2012). http://hbr.org/2012/11/mumbais-models-of-service-excellence/ar/1.

Wirzba, Norman. *Food & Faith: A Theology of Eating*. New York: Cambridge University Press, 2011.

Volck, Brian. "Late October Tomatoes." In *The Spirit of Food: 34 Writers on Feasting and Fasting Toward God*, edited by Leslie Leyland Fields, 8–15. Eugene, OR: Cascade, 2010.

Zimmerman, Steve. *Food in the Movies*. 2nd ed. Jefferson, NC: McFarland, 2010.

Filmography

Alamar. Directed by Pedro González-Rubio. 2009. New York, NY: Film Movement, 2011. DVD.

Angela's Ashes. Directed by Alan Parker. 1999. Hollywood, CA: Paramount Home Entertainment, 2000. DVD.

Babette's Feast. Directed by Gabriel Axel. 1987. New York, NY: The Criterion Collection, 2013. DVD, Blu-Ray.

Beasts of the Southern Wild. Directed by Benh Zeitlin. 2012. Los Angeles, CA: Fox Searchlight Pictures, 2012. DVD, Blu-Ray.

Big Night. Directed by Stanly Tucci, Campbell Scott. 1996. New York, NY: Sony Pictures Home Entertainment, 2002. DVD.

Chef. Directed by John Favreau. 2014. Los Angeles, CA: Universal Studios Home Entertainment, 2014. DVD, Blu-Ray.

Crying Ladies. Directed by Mark Meilly. 2003. Manila, Philippines: Unitel Pictures, 2014. DVD.

Departures. Directed by Takita Yôjirô. 2008. Toronto, Canada: E1 Entertainment, 2010. DVD.

Eat Drink Man Woman. Directed by Ang Lee. 1994. Beverly Hills, CA: MGM Home Entertainment, 2002. DVD.

Eat Pray Love. Directed by Ryan Murphy. 2010. New York, NY: Sony Pictures Home Entertainment, 2010. DVD, Blu-Ray.

Eatrip. Directed by Yuri Nomura. 2009. San Francisco, CA: New People Entertainment, 2011. DVD.

The Gleaners and I. Directed by Agnès Varda. 2000. New York, NY: Zeitgeist Video, 2002. DVD.

The Hundred-Foot Journey. Directed by Lasse Hallströ[set diaeresis over o]m. 2014. New York, NY: Walt Disney Studios, 2014. DVD, Blu-Ray.

ICHTHUS. Directed by Ton Sison. 2006. Chicago, IL: Antonio Sison. https://vimeo.com/139267591

Into the Wild. Directed by Sean Penn. 2007. Hollywood, CA: Paramount Home Entertainment, 2008. DVD.

Jiro Dreams of Sushi. Directed by David Gelb. 2011. New York, NY: Magnolia Pictures, 2012. DVD, Blu-Ray.

Julie and Julia. Directed by Nora Ephron. 2009. New York, NY: Sony Pictures Home Entertainment, 2009. DVD, Blu-Ray.

July Rhapsody. Directed by Ann Hui. 2001. Hong Kong: Tai Seng, 2006. DVD.

Like Water for Chocolate. Directed by Alfonso Arau. 1992. Santa Monica, CA: Miramax, 2011. DVD, Blu-Ray.

The Lunchbox. Directed by Ritesh Batra. 2013. New York, NY: Sony Pictures Home Entertainment, 2014. DVD, Blu-Ray.

Miracle of Marcelino/Marcelino Pan y Vino. Directed by Ladislao Vajda. 1955. Tulsa, OK: VCI Entertainment, 2010. DVD, Blu-Ray.

127 Hours. Directed by Danny Boyle. 2010. Los Angeles, CA: Fox Searchlight Pictures, 2011. DVD, Blu-Ray.

The Postmodern Life of my Aunt. Directed by Ann Hui. 2006. Hong Kong: Universe Laser, 2016. DVD.

The Scent of Green Papaya. Directed by Tranh Anh Hung. 1993. Culver City, CA: Columbia Tri-Star Home Entertainment, 2001. DVD.

A Simple Life. Directed by Ann Hui. 2011. Plano, TX: Well Go USA, 2013. DVD, Blu-Ray.

Spinning Plates. Directed by Joseph Levy. 2012. Sherman Oaks, CA: Inception Media Group, 2014. DVD.

Step up to the Plate. Directed by Paul Lacoste. 2012. New York, NY: Cinema Guild, 2013. DVD.

Tampopo. Directed by Juzo Itami. 1985. New York, NY: Fox Lorber Home Video, 1998. DVD.

Terms of Endearment. Directed by James L. Brooks. 1983. Burbank, CA: Warner Home Video, 2013. DVD, Blu-Ray.

Waltz with Bashir. Directed by Ari Folman. 2008. New York, NY: Sony Pictures Home Entertainment, 2009. DVD.

Whale Rider. Directed by Niki Caro. 2002. New York, NY: Columbia Tristar Home Entertainment, 2003. DVD, Blu-Ray.

Subject Index